ESSENTIAL LIFE SKILLS FOR YOUTH

The Life Skills Cookbook for Growing Minds

ESSENTIAL LIFE SKILLS
FOR YOUTH

THE LIFE SKILLS COOKBOOK FOR GROWING MINDS

RAFIQ KHAN, MD, PHD

Disclaimer:

No segment of this book might be replicated, disseminated, or transferred in any structure or using all means, comprising copying, recording, or mechanical or electronic techniques, or by any data stockpiling and recovery framework without the written consent of the author.

Notice of Liability:

The information provided in this book is provided without any warranty. The writer will not be liable to any individual or an entity with respect to any misfortunes or liabilities caused or asserted to be caused directly or indirectly by the content and the links provided in this book.

Imprint: Independently published

SOMETHING
FOR
YOU

GET A
COPY FOR

FREE

Scan QR Code to get
a FREE Copy

TABLE OF CONTENTS

WHY THIS BOOK?

It is never too early to start learning about the important skills that will help you navigate through life's ups and downs. As a child, you are constantly growing, developing, and discovering who you are and what you want to be. This is a critical time in your life, and I believe that by learning about essential life skills, you will be setting yourself up for a bright future filled with happiness and success.

For adolescents and teens, the acquisition of life skills is equally as crucial as academic achievement. A successful and meaningful life depends on having the necessary life skills, which include emotional intelligence, communication, critical thinking, problem solving, financial literacy, and health and wellbeing. Children can learn and practice these abilities from an early age, and they will benefit from having them throughout their life.

The book discusses the value of personal development, safety and emergency preparedness, social and emotional development, education and learning, career and professional development, personal finance and basic budgeting, mental health and stress management, essential life skills and basic computer skills and digital literacy. It also emphasizes the importance of problem-solving and critical thinking in academic and professional contexts. Along with providing helpful advice and direction for parents and educators on how to assist kids to enjoy healthy and financially secure lives, the book also covers financial literacy and health and wellness skills.

I offer a thorough manual for young people's life skill development in this book. The development of personal and social skills, academic and professional competencies, financial literacy, overall health and wellness and many more skills are all major areas of life skill development that are covered. The book is an invaluable tool for parents, educators, and anybody trying to educate kids because it covers every area of life skills development.

I urge you to read this book and learn about the crucial life skills to support you in achieving your objectives and leading the life you desire, whether you are just starting out or well on your way.

UNIQUE FEATURES AND STRUCTURE OF THIS BOOK

Age-appropriate language: Written in age-appropriate and simple language. This would make the book more interactive and hands-on for the reader.

Age-appropriate activities and exercises: To make the book more engaging and interactive, it incorporates age-appropriate activities that children can participate in to develop skills.

Comprehensive range of skills: Including real-life examples and case studies of children who have successfully developed and utilized these life skills would provide inspiration and motivation for readers.

Reflection exercises: Includes reflection exercises and prompts for readers to think about how they can apply what they have learned in their own lives could be a useful and unique feature.

Collaborative learning: Encouraging collaborative learning and group activities could be a unique feature that promotes teamwork and social skills development.

WHY SHOULD YOU READ THIS BOOK?

Dear young reader, I understand that you are growing up quickly and have many things happening in your life right now. You are learning new subjects at school, spending time with loved ones, and figuring out who you are and what you hope to become. That is why I believe it is particularly important for you to begin learning about essential life skills now.

These skills will help you navigate through the ups and downs of life. They will give you the tools to take care of yourself and build strong relationships with others. By reading this book on essential life skills, you will not only gain knowledge, but also a better understanding of yourself.

At this stage in your life, you have the ability to shape your future. By acquiring these valuable skills, you will be setting yourself up for both a successful future and a fulfilling present. And do not forget, it is never too late or too early to start learning. The more you know, the more control you have over your life and the future you want.

I know growing up can be challenging, but I have faith in you. Reading this book on essential life skills will help you establish a strong foundation for a happy and successful life. So, take that first step today and start reading. Your future self will thank you!

CHAPTER 1.

SAFETY AND EMERGENCY PREPAREDNESS

Safety rules, first aid, emergency preparedness, road safety, water safety, fire safety, internet safety, and basic survival skills

BASIC FIRST AID:

Understanding basic first aid techniques and knowing what to do in case of an emergency

First aid is when you help someone who is hurt or not feeling well. It is important for you to know some basic first aid so you can help if someone needs it. If someone is bleeding, put pressure on the wound with a cloth or bandage. If the bleeding will not stop, call for help. If someone is hurt and cannot move, do not move them. If someone is choking, give them back blows or abdominal thrusts. If someone is burned, cool the burn with water for 20 minutes. If someone feels faint or dizzy, help them lie down and raise their feet.

Remember to tell an adult if someone needs help and practice first aid skills often.

First aid is important to know in case of an emergency or injury. As a youngster, you should learn basic first aid skills.

ROAD SAFETY:

Understanding the rules and regulations of road safety and how to stay safe while walking, biking or driving.

Road safety is important to keep yourself and others safe when you are walking, biking or in a car. Here are some things to remember:

> ➢ Look both ways before crossing the street.
> ➢ Use the sidewalk or side of the road when walking or biking.
> ➢ Wear a helmet when biking or scootering.
> ➢ Wear a seatbelt when in a car.
> ➢ Do not walk or play in the street.
> ➢ Follow traffic lights and signs.
> ➢ Be careful around big vehicles like buses and trucks.
> ➢ Do not run into the street or chase things.
> ➢ Tell an adult where you are going if you are walking or biking.

Always be aware of your surroundings and follow the rules. Safety is the most important thing.

WATER SAFETY:

Understanding the basic rules of water safety and how to stay safe while swimming or boating.

Water safety is important to keep yourself and others safe when you are near or in water. Here are some simple tips to remember:

- ➢ Always ask permission from an adult before going near or in the water
- ➢ Never go swimming alone, always have a buddy with you
- ➢ Learn how to swim and be familiar with the water you are swimming in
- ➢ Wear a life jacket when boating or participating in water sports
- ➢ Follow all rules and safety guidelines at pools or other bodies of water
- ➢ Be aware of the weather and water conditions
- ➢ Learn basic water rescue techniques
- ➢ Do not swim if you are feeling tired or sick

Always follow the rules and stay alert. Remember, safety is the most important thing.

FIRE SAFETY:

Understanding the basic rules of fire safety and how to prevent and respond to fires.

Fire safety is very important to know. It means keeping ourselves and our families safe if there is a fire. Here are some things to remember:

- ➢ Never play with matches or lighters. They can start fires and hurt you
- ➢ Know about two ways out of your house in case of a fire
- ➢ Practice a fire drill at home so you know what to do if there is a fire
- ➢ Do not leave things like candles or cooking food alone
- ➢ Keep things that can catch on fire, like paper or cloths, away from hot things like stoves or heaters
- ➢ Keep bedroom and exit doors open, so you can get out easily if there is a fire
- ➢ Make sure you have smoke alarms in your house and know what they sound like
- ➢ If there is a fire, get out of the house immediately and call emergency fire brigade number

Remember, safety is the most important thing!

INTERNET SAFETY:

Understanding the risks of the internet and how to stay safe while online.

When you are on the internet, it is important to be aware of the information you share and the people you interact with. Here are some tips to help keep you safe online:

Be careful about the personal information you share online. This includes your name, address, phone number, and school. Keep this information private and only share it with people you know and trust.

Be aware of who you are talking to online. Not everyone is who they say they are, and it is important to be cautious when communicating with strangers.

Be mindful of what you post online. Remember that once something is on the internet, it is there forever and can be seen by many people.

Watch out for online scams. Some people may try to trick you into giving them personal information or money. Always be skeptical of unsolicited offers or requests for personal information.

Keep your passwords safe and never share them with anyone.

Do not click on links or download anything from people you do not know or trust.

If you come across something online that makes you feel uncomfortable or unsafe, tell a trusted adult right away.

It is important to be aware of what you are doing online and to always be safe. Remember, the internet is a great tool, but it is important to use it safely.

CYBERBULLYING:

Understanding the impact of cyberbullying and how to prevent it.

Cyberbullying is a serious issue that affects many young people today. It occurs when someone uses technology, such as the internet or a mobile phone, to hurt, threaten, or harass someone else. This can be very harmful to the person being bullied and can lead to serious problems, such as depression and anxiety.

It is important for you to understand what cyberbullying is and how to stay safe online. Here are some tips for avoiding cyberbullying:

Be careful about what you share online: Be mindful of the personal information you share online, like your address, phone number, or school name. This information can be used by cyberbullies to find and harm you.

Do not engage with cyberbullies: If someone is bullying you online, do not respond to their messages or comments. This can make the situation worse and give the cyberbully more power.

25

Block or report the cyberbully: If someone is bullying you online, you can block them, so you do not see their messages or comments. You can also report the cyberbully to the platform or website where the bullying is happening.

Tell someone you trust: If you are being cyberbullied, it is important to tell someone you trust, such as a parent, teacher, or friend. They can help you stay safe and find a solution to the problem.

Remember, cyberbullying is never okay. If you or someone you know is being cyberbullied, it is important to get help right away. By being aware of the dangers of cyberbullying and taking steps to stay safe online, you can help protect yourself and others from this harmful behavior.

DIGITAL CITIZENSHIP:

Understanding the rights and responsibilities of being a responsible digital citizen.

Digital citizenship refers to the moral and responsible use of technology and the internet. It is vital to understand the principles of digital citizenship and how they may impact your life and the lives of people around you.

One of the most essential aspects of digital citizenship is respect for others. This means that even while you are in front of a computer, you should not engage in gossip or speak negatively about people. It is important to behave civilly and respectfully toward others when using technology, just as you would in real life.

Protecting your personal data is a crucial component of digital citizenship. This includes refraining from giving strangers online access to private information like your home address or phone number. Using secure passwords and exercising caution when downloading attachments or clicking on links comes highly recommended.

Being a good digital citizen also entails being a responsible one. This entails being aware of how much time you are spending on your devices and refraining from wasting it online. It also means utilizing technology to benefit people and change the world for the better.

Last but not least, practicing digital citizenship also entails being aware of how technology affects the environment. This entails lowering your carbon footprint by turning off electronics when not in use and exercising awareness of how much paper and other resources you use.

In conclusion, digital citizenship plays a significant role in our lives nowadays. It is crucial for you to comprehend the fundamentals of digital citizenship and to put them into daily practice. You may have a positive influence on the world and the lives of those around you by acting as a responsible and courteous digital citizen.

BASIC SURVIVAL SKILLS:

Understanding the basics of survival skills such as building a fire, finding shelter and getting food and water

Basic survival skills are important for everyone to know, especially for youngsters. Here are a few basic survival skills that are easy for you to learn:

First, always carry a water bottle with you and make sure to drink plenty of water to stay hydrated. Second, always carry a flashlight with you, in case you get lost or need to see in the dark. Third, always carry a first aid kit with you, in case of injuries. Fourth, always carry a whistle with you, in case you need to signal for help. Fifth, always carry a map and compass with you, so you can navigate and find your way if you get lost. Remember, these are just a few basic survival skills, and it is always a good idea to learn more as you grow older.

Survival skills are important things for us to know. They can help us stay safe and take care of ourselves in different situations, like if we get lost in the woods or if there is a big storm. Three important survival skills are making a fire, finding a place to stay, and getting food and water.

Making a fire is a really important survival skill. It can keep us warm, dry, and safe. We can use it to cook food and even to tell people where we are. To make a fire, we need to find dry sticks, little twigs and something to start the fire with like matches or a special stick. We also need to make sure we're making the fire in a safe place, away from anything that can burn and with a big open space around it.

Finding a place to stay is another important survival skill. It can protect us from the rain or the sun. We can find a place to stay by using things from nature like rocks, trees or caves. We can also make a shelter using branches, leaves and other things from nature. We need to make sure the shelter is strong and not too close to any animals that might be dangerous.

Getting food and water is also really important for survival. We can get food by fishing, hunting or by picking wild berries and fruits. We need to make sure we know which plants and animals are safe to eat and which ones are not. We can get water from rivers, streams, or by catching rainwater. We need to make sure the water is clean and safe to drink before we drink it.

In conclusion, survival skills like making a fire, finding a place to stay, and getting food and water are important things for young person your age to know. They can help us stay safe and take care of ourselves in different situations. We should always pay attention to our surroundings and use these skills responsibly. And remember, if we ever get lost or in danger, we should stay calm and call for help.

EMERGENCY PREPAREDNESS:

Understanding the basics of emergency preparedness and how to prepare for natural disasters.

Basic emergency preparedness is important for you to know, so that you can stay safe during unexpected events like storms, earthquakes, or fires. Here are some things we can do to be prepared:

Learn emergency phone numbers: Make sure you know the phone number of emergency services like 911 and your parents' or guardians' numbers, so that you can call for help in case of an emergency.

Make an emergency plan: Talk to your family and make a plan on what to do in case of an emergency. This can include where to meet up, how to communicate, and what to do if you are separated.

Keep an emergency kit: Have a bag or container with basic emergency supplies like water, non-perishable food, a flashlight, a first aid kit and a whistle.

Know the emergency exits: Learn the emergency exits in your home and at school, so that you know how to get out quickly and safely in case of an emergency.

Learn basic safety tips: Learn basic safety tips like Stop, Drop, and Roll in case of a fire, and how to get low and cover your head during an earthquake.

Be aware of your surroundings: Always be aware of what is happening around you and pay attention to any emergency alerts or warnings that are given.

Remember, being prepared for emergencies can help us stay safe and take care of ourselves and others during unexpected events. It is important to practice emergency preparedness regularly and always be aware of our surroundings.

EMERGENCY RESPONSE SKILLS:

Understanding the basics of emergency response and how to stay safe and help others in case of an emergency

It is important to be prepared for emergencies by knowing your phone number and address, how to call for help, what to do in different types of emergencies, and having a plan with your family. Practice your plan and stay calm during an emergency and listen to grown-ups for instructions.

It is important for you to know what to do in case of an emergency. Here are some things you should remember:

Know your phone number and address so you can call Emergency Response Team such as 911 or tell someone where you live.

Learn how to use a phone to call emergency number, and also how to call your parents or a trusted adult.

Know what to do in different emergencies. For example, if there is a fire, get out of the building and call 911. If there is a storm, go to a safe place like a basement or designated shelter.

Make a plan with your family on what to do in case of emergencies. This should include a meeting place outside your home in case you get separated and a way to contact each other.

Practice your emergency plan so you know what to do.

Stay calm and not panic if an emergency happens. Remember to take deep breaths and follow your emergency plan.

Listen to grown-ups and follow their instructions in an emergency. They will help keep you safe.

By doing these things, you will be better prepared to handle any emergency that may happen.

Difference between emergency preparedness and emergency response:

Emergency preparedness is all about getting ready for an emergency before it happens. This includes things like making a plan with your family, practicing that plan, and knowing important phone numbers and addresses. It is like getting ready for a big test or a sports game - you want to make sure you know what to do and have everything you need before the emergency happens.

Emergency response, on the other hand, is what you do when an emergency is actually happening. This includes things like staying calm, following your emergency plan, and listening to grown-ups. It is like when the test or game actually starts - you use what you've prepared to handle the situation.

Think of it like a fire drill at school. Before the drill, the teachers will talk to you about what to do in case of a fire and practice with you, so you know how to evacuate safely. During the drill, you put that practice into action and leave the building. That is like emergency preparedness and response.

EXERCISE ACTIVITY 1

EXERCISE ACTIVITY 1
"BUILD AN EMERGENCY KIT"

Objective:

To teach children about the importance of being prepared for emergencies and how to create their own emergency kit.

Materials:

A large box or storage container
A list of essential items for an emergency kit (flashlight, batteries, first aid kit, bottled water, non-perishable food, etc.)
Blank paper and pencils

Instructions

Step 1:
Start by creating an emergency kit. Gather a few supplies such as a flashlight, batteries, a first aid kit, bottled water, and non-perishable food. Place these items in a large box or storage container.

Step 2:
Think about different emergency scenarios, such as a natural disaster, power outage, or medical emergency.

Step 3:
Discuss with an adult or another trusted person what you would do in each scenario. Make sure to have a plan for how to stay safe and reach for help if needed.

Step 4:
Practice the emergency response plan by role-playing different scenarios with a trusted adult or friend.

Step 5:
Reflect on what you learned from this exercise and what you would do to be better prepared for emergencies in the future.

EXERCISE ACTIVITY 2

EXERCISE ACTIVITY 2
"SAFETY SCENARIO SIMULATION"

Objective:

To help children understand and practice emergency preparedness and safety skills.

Materials:

A large open space, props such as chairs, tables, and pillows, index cards, and pens.

Instructions (Group activity)

Divide the children into small groups of 2-3.

Give each group an index card and a pen.
Instruct each group to write down a different emergency scenario, such as a fire, an earthquake, or a power outage.

Have each group act out their scenario, using props such as chairs and tables to simulate a building or home.
While the groups are acting out their scenarios, the rest of the kids will be the "rescuers" and will need to assess the situation and respond appropriately.

After each scenario, have a group discussion about what was done correctly and what could be improved upon in terms of emergency preparedness and safety.
Repeat the activity with different scenarios and different groups of kids taking turns as rescuers.

Conclude the activity by reviewing the importance of being prepared and knowing how to respond in an emergency. Emphasize that practicing these skills can help keep them safe in real-life situations.

EXERCISE ACTIVITY 3

EXERCISE ACTIVITY 3
"CYBER SAFETY ADVENTURE"

Objective:

To educate children on the dangers of cyberbullying and how to stay safe online.

Materials:

- A computer or tablet
- Internet access
- A pen and paper

Instructions (Group activity)

- Start by explaining to the child what cyberbullying is and why it's harmful. Show examples of cyberbullying behavior and emphasize the importance of treating others online with kindness and respect.
- Have the child navigate to a website that provides information on internet safety and cyberbullying, such as the National Cyber Security Alliance or StopBullying.gov.
- Have the child take notes on the tips and strategies provided for staying safe online and avoiding cyberbullying. Encourage the child to ask questions and discuss their thoughts and concerns.
- Together, create a "Cyber Safety Plan" that outlines the child's personal strategies for staying safe online and avoiding cyberbullying. This could include setting privacy settings, not responding to negative comments or messages, and reporting any incidents of cyberbullying to a trusted adult.
- Practice scenario-based problem solving by role playing different situations that the child may encounter online, such as receiving a mean message or seeing a friend being bullied. Encourage the child to use their Cyber Safety Plan and the strategies they learned to respond appropriately.
- Finally, encourage the child to share their new knowledge with friends and family and to continue to educate themselves on internet safety and cyberbullying.

CHAPTER 2.

PERSONAL DEVELOPMENT

Personal hygiene, manners, emotions, problem-solving, time management, money management, self-care, and. personal values, self-esteem

Personal development is about becoming the best version of yourself. It is like building a house: you start with the basics, like taking care of your body, being polite and understanding your emotions. Then more complex things are added, such as solving problems, managing time and money, and taking care of oneself. It is important to keep building and growing so that you can be proud of who you are. Personal development also includes self-esteem, which is how you feel about yourself and how you think others see you. It is important to have a positive self-esteem to be happy and have self-confidence. In general, personal development is about becoming the best version of yourself, both inside and out.

PERSONAL GROOMING:

Understanding the basics of personal grooming and how to maintain a polished appearance.

Personal grooming is like giving yourself a mini makeover every day! To take care of yourself, you should brush your teeth, wash your face, and comb your hair. It is also important to wear clean clothes and keep them clean. When you take care of yourself, you will feel good and look good too. So, remember to take care of yourself every day!

PERSONAL HYGIENE:

The importance of regular hand washing, brushing teeth, bathing, grooming, and general cleanliness.

Maintaining personal hygiene is crucial in ensuring both physical and mental well-being. Basic habits such as washing hands regularly, brushing teeth, bathing, grooming and keeping yourself clean, helps in preventing the spread of germs and illnesses. Consistently following these habits can also enhance your self-confidence and self-esteem, as well as make a positive impression on others. It is crucial for you to learn the importance of personal hygiene at an early age, so that it becomes a habitual practice throughout your life.

PERSONAL BRANDING:

Understanding the basics of personal branding and how to promote oneself effectively.

Personal branding is all about how people see you and what they think of you. It is like making a logo for yourself! Just like a company has a logo to tell people what they are all about, you also have a brand that tells people who you are and what you stand for. Some ways to promote yourself and make a good brand for yourself include being kind, being helpful, and doing your best in everything you do. It is also important to be true to yourself and be proud of who you are. When you have a good brand, people will think well of you and want to be friends with you or work with you. So, make sure to be the best version of yourself and promote yourself in a positive way!

SELF-ESTEEM:

Understanding the basics of self-esteem and how to build and maintain it.

Self-esteem is how you feel about yourself. Sometimes, you might hear a voice in your head that says mean things, but it is important to learn to make that voice be nice. You can make yourself feel good by doing things like trying your best in school, being kind to others, and taking care of your body. It is also good to be around people who make you feel good about yourself, and not listen to mean voice in your head.

Remember, you are special and deserve to feel good about yourself.

TIME MANAGEMENT:

Understanding the basics of time management and how to prioritize tasks and manage time efficiently.

Time management is all about being in charge of how you spend your time. It is like being the boss of your own time! When you learn how to manage your time, you can make sure you use it efficiently and accomplish all the things you want to do.

One important part of time management is learning how to prioritize your tasks. This means doing the most important things first and saving the less important things for later. For example, if you have homework to do, you should do that before you play video games.

Another important part of time management is breaking down big tasks into smaller tasks. This makes it easier to manage and accomplish. For example, if you have a big project to do for school, you can break it down into smaller tasks like research, writing, and editing.

It is also important to set a schedule for yourself and stick to it. This means making a plan of what you want to do and when you want to do it. This can help you stay organized and on track.

45

In summary, time management is all about being in charge of your own time, prioritizing your tasks, breaking down big tasks into smaller tasks and setting a schedule for yourself and sticking to it. Remember, time is a precious resource, we cannot get it back once it is gone, so it's important to use it wisely!

Personal Values:

Understanding one's personal values and beliefs and how they shape one's actions and decisions.

Personal values are things that are important to you. They help you make good choices and be kind to others. Examples of personal values are honesty, kindness, respect, and responsibility. It is important to think about your values and make sure they are things that truly matter to you. Everyone's values are different and that is okay. We should respect and accept others for who they are and their personal values. Understanding your own personal values helps you make good choices and be the best version of yourself. We can learn and grow our values as we get older.

Personal values are most important to us. They are like special rules that we follow to make sure we make good choices and treat others nicely. Some examples of personal values are being honest, kind, respectful and responsible.

When we understand our personal values, it helps us make good choices. Like if honesty is one of our values, we will always tell the truth and never lie. And if kindness is one of our values, we will be kind to others and help them when they need it.

47

It is important to think about our values and make sure they are things that are truly important to us. We can do this by thinking about what matters to us and what we believe in. This can help us understand our values and beliefs better.

It is also important to remember that everyone's values are different. Just because someone else's values are different from ours, it does not mean they are wrong. We should respect and accept people for who they are and their personal values.

So, personal values are really important because they help us make good choices, treat others with respect, and be the best version of ourselves. As we grow up, we can learn new values and make them a part of our lives.

GOAL-SETTING:

Setting and working towards personal goals and aspirations.

Setting goals is similar to creating a plan for the things you wish to do or possess. When you achieve your goal, it makes you feel content and proud, and it keeps you motivated and focused. It is similar to creating a wish list and working out how to fulfill your desires. For instance, if you wanted to learn how to ride a bike, your plan might be to practice riding a bike every day in order to achieve your objective. Setting objectives will help you improve your future and add more joy and excitement to your life.

Goal setting is when you make a plan for something you want to do or have, and then follow the plan to make it happen. It helps you stay focused and motivated to do something you really want.

Do you know what a goal is? A goal is something that you want to achieve or accomplish. It's like a dream that you want to make come true. Setting goals is important because it helps us know what we want to do and helps us work towards it.

49

For example, if your goal is to be a doctor, you have to study hard and learn a lot about the human body and medicine. And once you achieve your goal of becoming a doctor, you will be able to help a lot of people and make them feel better.

Setting goals helps us stay focused and gives us something to work towards. It is important to set small goals and big goals, and as you achieve them, you'll feel proud of yourself and motivated to keep going.

In conclusion, setting goals is an important thing to do. It helps us focus on what we want to do and gives us something to work towards. Keep setting goals and working hard to achieve them, and you will be proud of yourself and all that you can accomplish.

SELF-CARE:

The importance of self-care, such as getting enough sleep, eating well, and managing stress.

Self-care is taking care of yourself, so you can feel good and be healthy. It is important to get enough sleep, eat healthy foods, and manage stress. Getting enough sleep helps your body rest and be ready for the next day. Eating healthy foods gives your body the energy and nutrients it needs to work well. Managing stress helps you feel calm and not overwhelmed. Think of it like keeping a healthy balance in your body and mind, like keeping a plant well-watered, so it can grow and be healthy.

It is important to do things that make us happy and keep our bodies and minds strong.

One way to take care of yourself is by getting enough sleep. Sleeping helps your body rest and be ready for the next day. Just like how you need to charge your tablet to play with it, you need to give your body a rest to be able to play and learn. Make sure you have a bedtime routine that helps you relax before bed, like reading a story or listening to calming music.

51

Another way to take care of yourself is by eating healthy foods. Eating fruits, vegetables, and other healthy foods gives our bodies the energy and nutrients it needs to work well. Try to eat a variety of foods and have something from each food group (like fruits, vegetables, grains and proteins).

Lastly, it is important to manage stress. Sometimes things happen that can make you feel upset or worried, like getting in trouble or having a fight with a friend. But it is important to find ways to calm down and feel better. You can talk to someone you trust, like your parents or a teacher, or do something you enjoy like drawing or playing with a toy. It is important to find something that works for you so that you can feel calm and not overwhelmed.

In summary, self-care is all about taking care of yourself so that you can feel good and be healthy.

PROBLEM-SOLVING:

Strategies for solving problems and resolving conflicts, including critical thinking and effective communication.

Problem solving is like trying to figure out how to solve a puzzle or a game. It is like trying to find the missing piece or the right way to make everything fit together. Sometimes it can be hard, but by breaking it down into smaller parts, looking for clues, using our imagination, and not giving up, you can find the solution. It is like being a detective and trying to solve a mystery! And if you do not figure it out right away, that's okay, you can always try again and learn from your mistakes.

Break the problem down into smaller parts: Try to understand each part of the problem and how they relate to each other.

Look for patterns: Identify patterns in the problem and use them to find a solution.

Use your imagination: Think creatively and come up with new and unique ideas to solve the problem.

Try different approaches: Don't be afraid to try multiple ways of solving the problem. One may not work, but another might work.

Practice: The more you practice problem-solving, the better you will become at it.

Do not give up: If you get stuck, take a break, and come back to the problem later. Persistence pays off.

Learn from your mistakes: If you do not find the solution, learn from your mistakes and try again.

Work with others: Collaborate with others to solve the problem, as two heads are often better than one.

RESPONSIBILITY:

The importance of being responsible for one's actions and taking ownership of one's decisions.

Everybody should possess the quality of responsibility. It entails taking responsibility for your own choices, actions, and results. There are various ways to develop responsibility. Here are a few of them:

You undoubtedly have a lot of valuables such as electronic gadgets, books, toys, games, etc. that you need to take care of. Being responsible for these things and keeping them structured is a terrific sign of that.

Making your bed, clearing the table after a meal, and doing the laundry are just a few examples of domestic activities that can help you learn responsibility.

Rules-following: Being responsible requires conforming to rules and boundaries whether at home, school, or while playing with friends.

Maintaining your word: If you make a promise, such as to assist a friend with their homework or arrive on time for a playdate, it is critical to maintain it.

Being truthful: Being accountable for your deeds and errors is a crucial component of being responsible. Own up to your mistakes and take action to put things right.

You can acquire and develop the critical skill of responsibility by modeling these behaviors. They will benefit from it in their daily lives as well as lay the groundwork for a prosperous future.

CRITICAL THINKING:

The ability to analyze and evaluate information and make informed decisions.

A crucial skill that aids in better decision-making and problem-solving is critical thinking. It is the capacity to analyze a situation thoroughly, objectively, and from all possible perspectives before coming to a judgment. Here are some pointers to get you going on strengthening your critical thinking abilities:

Pose queries: Ask questions and learn as much as you can about a topic without being hesitant. Making an informed decision will be easier with a greater understanding of the issue or circumstance.

Think from a variety of angles: Attempt to approach a situation from many angles. This will enable you to explore all your options and view the problem from several perspectives.

Analyze the evidence: Taken into account facts and evidence while making decisions. Before making a choice, carefully assemble all necessary data and consider the available facts.

Look for patterns and relationships: When attempting to solve a problem, search for patterns and relationships. This will assist you in better comprehending the issue and developing a solution.

Experiment with unconventional thinking: Don't be scared to think outside the box and generate fresh concepts. Sometimes the most creative and original idea is the best one.

You will become a better problem-solver and make better decisions in everyday life by developing your critical thinking abilities.

BASIC MANNERS:

Saying "please" and "thank you," not interrupting when someone is speaking, not talking with their mouths full, showing respect to others, and being polite.

Manners are the polite things we do and say to show respect to others. They help us get along with others and make the world a nicer place to be in. Here are some basic manners that are important for you to learn:

Saying "please" and "thank you" is a very important manner. When you ask for something, you should always say "please" and when someone gives you something or does something for you, you should always say "thank you." It is a simple way to show that you appreciate what others do for you.

Being respectful to adults is also a manner that is important to learn. You should always use polite words when talking to adults and look at them when they are talking to us. We should also listen carefully when adults are talking and not interrupt them.

Table manners are also important. At mealtimes, you should use utensils properly, and not talk with your mouth full. You should also ask to be excused when we want to leave the table.

Waiting your turn is also important. When you are playing a game or waiting in line, you should wait patiently for your turn and not push in front of others.

Another important manner is to be kind and considerate of others. You should always be nice and helpful to others and think about how your actions may affect others.

By learning and practicing these manners, you can show respect and kindness to others and make the world a better place. Remember, manners are like magic words that can open many doors and make people happy, it is a small effort for a big impact.

EXERCISE ACTIVITY 4

EXERCISE ACTIVITY 4
"MIRROR TALK REFLECTION"

Objective:

To help kids reflect on their personal development and identify areas for growth.

Materials:

- A mirror and a pen and paper for each child

Instructions

- Stand in front of a mirror and look at your reflection.
- Think about your personality traits, strengths, and weaknesses.
- Write down what you see in your reflection.
- Share your thoughts with a partner or in a small group.
- What would you like to improve or develop in yourself? Set achievable goals in those areas.
- Reflect on your progress regularly and make changes as needed.

EXERCISE ACTIVITY 5

EXERCISE ACTIVITY 5
"MY TIME JAR"

Objective:

To educate children on time management, and become more productive and efficient.

Materials:

- A large glass jar or container
- small pieces of paper, and
- pen or pencil.

Instructions

- Label the jar "My Time Jar."
- Set a timer for 10 minutes.
- Think about all the activities you did in the past day.
- For each activity, write it down on a small piece of paper and put it in the jar.
- Continue until the timer goes off or all activities are listed.
- Remove all the papers from the jar and sort them into two piles: "Important" and "Not as important."
- Take a look at the "Important" pile and think about how much time you spent on each activity.
- Think about how you can prioritize the "Important" activities in the future to make the most of your time.
- Think about ways you can limit or eliminate the "Not as important" activities so you can have more time for the things that matter most.
- Write down your thoughts and ideas in a notebook or journal.
- This activity can be done on a regular basis to help you track your time and develop better time management skills. By reflecting on your activities, you will gain a better understanding of how you are using your time and what changes you can make to be more productive and efficient.

EXERCISE ACTIVITY 6

EXERCISE ACTIVITY 6 "CRITICAL THINKING AND PROBLEM-SOLVING"

Objective:

To help you develop critical thinking and problem-solving skills.

Materials:

- Pen and paper for each child.

Instructions

- Think about a common problem that you often face, such as difficulty in understanding a concept, not being able to focus, or forgetting to turn in homework.
- Write down the problem at the top of a blank sheet of paper.
- Brainstorm five potential solutions to the problem.
- Think creatively and outside the box.
- Evaluate each solution and choose the best one.
- Write a plan of action for implementing the chosen solution.
- Finally, reflect on the process and what you learned about critical thinking and problem-solving.

Note: This exercise can be repeated with different problems to further strengthen critical thinking and problem-solving skills.

CHAPTER 3.

PHYSICAL HEALTH

Physical health refers to the overall well-being of the body. It includes having a healthy diet, getting enough exercise, and getting enough sleep. It also includes taking care of any physical illnesses or injuries and visiting the doctor for regular check-ups. Having good physical health means that our bodies are strong, flexible, and able to perform daily activities with ease. It also means that we have a good immune system which helps us to fight off illnesses and diseases. Overall, physical health is important for maintaining a high quality of life and being able to do the things we enjoy.

NUTRITION:

The importance of a balanced diet, the food groups, and how to make healthy choices.

By eating **wholesome meals**, you can take care of your body through nutrition. To make sure that your body receives all the nutrients required for growth and wellness, you must eat a range of foods. Following are some fundamental concepts in nutrition:

Vegetables and fruits are necessary for a healthy diet. They are a great source of nutrients, vitamins, and antioxidants that help keep your body healthy. The greatest method to ensure you are getting all the nutrients your body requires is to eat a variety of fruits and vegetables.

A diet that is balanced must include grains. They are present in many different foods, including pasta, bread, cereal, and rice. Our body runs on grain, which also fosters growth. Eating whole grains, such as whole wheat bread or brown rice, is the greatest way to consume grains and get the most nutrition from them.

Proteins are an additional requirement for a healthy diet. Beef, shellfish, beans, and nuts are some of the foods that contain them. Proteins are used by our bodies to build and repair muscles and other tissues. Eating a variety of different proteins is the best way to get all the nutrients our bodies need.

Dairy products like milk and cheese are necessary for a balanced diet. They have adequate levels of calcium, which is essential for strong bones and teeth. Water consumption is also crucial. To remain hydrated and healthy, our bodies require water.

Maintaining balance in your diet and avoiding eating too much or too little of anything is also crucial. In order to receive all the nutrients you require, try to consume a variety of foods from each food group.

You may feel good, have energy to play and learn, and grow strong and healthy by eating wholesome foods and maintaining a balanced diet, which is crucial for your general health and wellbeing. Keep in mind that food serves as our body's fuel, making it crucial to select the proper kind.

PHYSICAL ACTIVITY:

The importance of regular exercise, different types of physical activities, and how to maintain a healthy lifestyle.

Physical activity is important for our bodies and minds. It helps us stay healthy and strong, and it is also a lot of fun! Here are some reasons why regular physical activity is important:

Regular physical activity helps our bodies stay strong and healthy. It helps our muscles and bones grow strong and it helps us stay at a healthy weight. It also helps our hearts and lungs work better, which is important for good health.

Regular physical activity can help you feel good. When you are physically active, your body release chemicals called endorphins, which makes you feel happy and energized.

Regular physical activity can help you sleep better. When you are physically active during the day, you feel more tired at night and sleep better.

Regular physical activity can also help you focus better and improve your memory. When you exercise, your brain gets more oxygen and this can help you think and learn better.

Regular physical activity is fun! There are so many different ways to be active, like playing sports, riding bikes, dancing, or going for a walk. You can find something you like to do, and it does not feel like work.

It is important to make physical activity a regular part of your daily routine, like going for a walk, bike ride or playing a game of tag with friends, it can be a fun way to stay active and healthy. Remember, physical activity is like taking a shower for your body, it is important to do it regularly to stay clean and fresh.

EXERCISE ACTIVITY 7

EXERCISE ACTIVITY 7
"BUILDING A HEALTHY HABITS
ROUTINE"

Objective:

To help you understand the importance of physical health and create healthy habits.

Materials:

- Pencil or pen
- notebook or journal, and
- a calendar or planner

Instructions

- Reflect on your current physical health habits. Do you regularly engage in physical activity? Do you eat nutritious foods?
- List at least three habits you would like to develop to improve your physical health.
- Use a calendar or planner to schedule a time for each of these habits into your daily routine.
- Stick to your schedule for at least a week.
- After a week, reflect on how these habits have affected your physical health. Have you seen any improvement?
- Finally, continue to develop healthy habits and make adjustments to your routine as needed.

Note: This activity can be repeated every few weeks or months to continue promoting healthy habits and reflection on physical health.

CHAPTER 4.

SOCIAL AND EMOTIONAL DEVELOPMENT

Empathy, diversity, cultural awareness, communication, social skills, conflict resolution, teamwork, and leadership

Your social and emotional growth is crucial because it aids in the understanding and control of your emotions, the formation and maintenance of relationships, and the growth of your sense of self. The following justifies the significance of social and emotional development:

Your social and emotional development aids in your understanding and control of your emotions. It teaches you how to deal with challenging emotions like impatience or grief and how to express your emotions in suitable ways.

Your social and emotional growth aids in the establishment and maintenance of connections. It enables you to develop social skills, make friends, and comprehend social cues and expectations.

Your sense of self-development is aided by your social and emotional growth. It aids in your understanding of who you are, your likes and dislikes, and your principles. Additionally, it aids in the development of self-confidence and self-esteem, both of which are crucial for feeling good about oneself.

Children who are socially and emotionally developed perform better in school and throughout their life. Children who are emotionally and socially mature are more likely to succeed in school, form satisfying relationships, and pursue rewarding occupations.

Children are happier and healthier when they are developing socially and emotionally. Positive relationships and a better existence are more likely to occur in children who have good social and emotional skills.

Social and emotional growth require nurturing and encouragement; they do not just happen automatically. This can be accomplished by having a secure and encouraging environment, setting an example of good social and emotional behavior, and availing opportunity to use and improve your social and emotional abilities. Encourage yourself to communicate your emotions, play with friends, and treat others with kindness and respect.

EMOTIONS:

Understanding and expressing emotions in a healthy way, as well as empathy towards others.

Our bodies and minds experience emotions, which are feelings. They may be pleasant emotions like joy and excitement or unpleasant emotions like sadness and rage. What you should know about emotions is as follows:

Humans experience emotions naturally and on a regular basis. Everyone experiences emotions, and it is critical to keep in mind that it is acceptable to feel both pleasant and bad feelings.

Emotions might be powerful or subdued. Our emotions can be strong at times, such as when we are extremely pleased or sad, but they can also be more subdued.

Emotions can shift abruptly. Sometimes we have a brief period of feeling one way before our emotions change.

Different methods can be used to express emotions. When they are depressed, some people may cry, while others may become enraged. When they are joyful, some people may laugh, while others may smile. Remember that there are both appropriate and inappropriate ways to express emotions.

Dizzying emotions are common. Sometimes we may be unsure about the reasons behind our feelings or what to do about them. That is alright. It is normal to have concerns and to not fully comprehend our emotions.

Understanding emotions can be challenging, but it is crucial to keep in mind that it is normal to experience a wide range of emotions and that it is crucial to learn how to control and express them in healthy ways. Express your emotions in words, seek assistance when necessary, and have compassion for yourself as you become more aware of your feelings.

CIVIC ENGAGEMENT:

Understanding one's role and responsibilities as a citizen, including voting and participating in community events.

Civic engagement is when people take part in activities that help make their community a better place. It can include things like voting in elections, volunteering at a local organization, or speaking up about issues that are important to you. You may think that you are too young to make a difference, but that is not true! There are many ways that you can get involved and make a positive impact in your community.

One way to get involved is by volunteering at a local organization. This could be a kitchen, a library, or a park. You can help out with tasks like sorting books, planting flowers, or serving food. Not only will you be helping others, but you will also be learning new skills and making new friends.

Another way to get involved is by joining a club or group that focuses on a cause you care about. For example, if you are passionate about animals, you could join a club at your school that raises money for animal shelters. Or if you are interested in the environment, you could participate in a local clean-up event. By joining these groups, you will be able to make a difference in areas you care about and learn more about them.

Another way to get involved is by speaking up about issues that are important to you. This could be something like writing a letter to your local government officials about a problem in your community or speaking to your classmates about a topic you are passionate about. By using your voice, you can raise awareness and make a change.

Civic engagement is important because it helps make our community a better place for everyone. You may think that you're too young to make a difference, but that's not true! There are many ways that you can get involved and make a positive impact in your community. Whether it is through volunteering, joining a club or group, or speaking up about issues that are important to you, you can make a difference.

COMMUNICATION:

The importance of effective communication and the different forms of communication, including non-verbal communication.

The capacity to effectively exchange information and ideas with others is referred to as communication skills. They are crucial because they enable us to interact with people and develop bonds with them. Good communication skills can have a significant impact on how people see you and how well you get along with others, whether you are speaking to friends, family, or teachers.

You may hone your communication skills in a variety of ways. Being a good listener is among the most crucial skills. This is listening carefully and trying to comprehend what people are saying. It also entails remaining silent and posing inquiries to demonstrate your interest.

Being precise and succinct in your speech is another approach to enhance your communication abilities. This entails speaking in plain, uncomplicated terms and refraining from using complex or unfamiliar phrases. It also entails speaking your mind and feeling honestly and plainly.

Becoming more conscious of your body language is another approach to enhance your communication abilities. This entails maintaining eye contact, grinning, and adopting an approachable and open body stance. It also entails being conscious of how your voice tone can impact the meaning you are attempting to convey.

In conclusion, effective communication is crucial for establishing trusting bonds and getting along with others. You may hone your communication skills and leave a favorable impression on others by being a good listener, communicating clearly and succinctly, and being conscious of your body language. Always keep in mind that communication is a two-way street, so when speaking or listening, be respectful and attentive.

CULTURAL AWARENESS:

Understanding and respecting different cultures and traditions.

Understanding and valuing people from various cultural backgrounds' way of life, traditions, and beliefs is known as cultural awareness. It is significant because it fosters an appreciation for the diversity of our environment and a recognition of the individuality of each person. We may learn from others and create communities that are more inclusive and robust by being culturally conscious.

Reading books, watching movies, and listening to music from other nations are some ways you learn about various cultures. This can provide you with a window into the traditions, practices, and morals of people from other origins.

Speaking with individuals from other backgrounds is another technique to gain knowledge of various cultures.

You can enquire with them about their traditions, beliefs, and practices. Additionally, you might inquire about their preferred meals, tunes, and occasions.

Additionally, going to cultural centers and museums can teach you about various civilizations. These locations feature events and displays that can instruct you about the history and culture of many ethnic communities.

Participating in festivals and events related to foreign cultures is another method to learn about them. This can be a wonderful way to get a personal taste of various cuisines, music, and cultures.

In summary, cultural awareness is crucial because it enables us to recognize and value the diversity in our world. We can create communities that are more resilient and inclusive if we educate ourselves about various cultures. There are numerous ways to get knowledge about various cultures, including reading books, conversing with people from various backgrounds, visiting museums, and taking part in cultural activities. Keep in mind that everyone is unique, and that by learning about various cultures, we can all benefit from one another and develop as people.

DIVERSITY:

The importance of accepting and valuing diversity in people and communities.

Diversity refers to the wide variety of individuals in the globe, each of whom has distinct traits, cultures, and origins. Understanding and valuing diversity is crucial because it improves and enriches both our communities and the wider world.

Learning about other cultures and backgrounds is one approach to accept diversity. Reading books, watching movies, and listening to music from other nations can all help you achieve this. You can also converse with folks from other origins and inquire about their traditions and rituals.

Being accepting of those who are different from you and having an open mind are two additional ways to embrace variety. This is refraining from making snap judgments or assumptions about individuals based on their color, ethnicity, religion, or any other trait. Additionally, it entails treating everyone with respect and kindness.

TEAMWORK:

The importance of working well with others and being a good team player.

When a group of people cooperates to accomplish a common objective, this is called teamwork. It is significant because it enables us to achieve more than we could independently. Working together, we may pool our talents, ideas, and resources to accomplish something truly amazing.

Effective communication is one trait of a team member. This is conversing with others, paying attention to what they have to say, contributing your own thoughts, and raising queries as necessary. Everyone can stay in sync and work toward the same objective with the aid of effective communication.

Being dependable is another trait that makes a strong team player. This entails being on time, contributing, and carrying out your obligations. The team can trust each other and function more effectively when everyone is reliable.

Being adaptable is another quality that makes a strong team player. This entails being open to altering your ideas or trying something new if it will benefit the team. The team can be more inventive and adaptable by being flexible.

Respecting and being kind to others is another approach to be a successful team player. This entails showing respect to everyone and having empathy for their sentiments. The team can function more effectively together when everyone acts with decency and respect.

In conclusion, teamwork is crucial since it enables us to achieve more than we could individually. We can all be terrific team players and accomplish great things together if we communicate clearly, are dependable, adaptable, and kind to others. Keep in mind that we can do more as a team than we can working separately.

SOCIAL SKILLS:

Understanding and navigating social interactions and relationships.

Social skills are the ways we interact with other people. They are important because they help us build relationships, make friends, and navigate different social situations. Good social skills can make our lives more enjoyable and fulfilling.

One way to develop good social skills is to practice good manners. This means saying "please" and "thank you", using "excuse me" when you need to interrupt, and being polite in general. Good manners show respect for others and help us to get along well with others.

Another way to develop good social skills is to be a good listener. This means paying attention when someone is talking, asking questions to show you are interested, and not interrupting. Being a good listener helps us to understand and connect with others.

You can also develop good social skills by being empathetic. This means putting yourself in other people's shoes and understanding how they feel. Being empathetic helps us to be kind and understanding towards others.

Another way to develop good social skills is by being confident. This means being comfortable in different social situations, speaking up when you have something to say, and being yourself. Being confident helps us to make friends, share our ideas and be ourselves.

Social skills are important because they help us build relationships, make friends and navigate different social situations. By practicing good manners, being a good listener, being empathetic and confident, we can develop good social skills that will make our lives more enjoyable and fulfilling. Remember, social skills are like muscles, the more you use them, the stronger they become.

CONFLICT RESOLUTION:

Understanding different methods of resolving conflicts and maintaining healthy relationships.

When two or more people disagree or have a problem with one another, there is a conflict. It is a common occurrence that can take place anywhere, whether at home, school, or with friends. However, it is crucial to understand how to settle disputes in a constructive and efficient manner.

Discussing the issue is one technique to settle disputes. This is being open and honest about your emotions, paying attention to the viewpoint of the other person, and making an effort to comprehend their perspective. You can discover a solution that works for everyone by discussing the issue.

Making a compromise is another method for resolving disputes. Finding a just solution for all parties concerned entails this. Finding a solution that everyone can support could include sacrificing something you desire.

Using "I" statements is another way to settle disputes. Instead of blaming or criticizing the other person, this entails discussing your own needs and feelings. You may say, for instance, "I get unhappy when we have to wait for you," as opposed to "you are always late."

Asking a third person who is impartial for assistance is another method for resolving disputes. This might be a parent, a teacher, or another responsible adult. They can assist you and the other person in comprehending one another's viewpoints and coming up with a solution.

Conflict occurs frequently in life, but it's crucial to understand how to handle them well. We can come up with answers that satisfy everyone by discussing the issue, negotiating, utilizing "I" expressions, and asking an impartial third party for assistance. Keep in mind that conflict resolution is a talent that can be acquired and developed with practice.

Rafiq Khan, MD, PhD

BASIC SIGN LANGUAGE:

Understanding the basics of sign language, including basic communication and grammar.

Hand gestures, facial expressions, and body language are all used in sign language to convey meaning. Anyone may learn it, and while those who are deaf or hard of hearing utilize it, it is also a pleasant and helpful skill.

Learning the alphabet is the first step in mastering the foundational signs of sign language. Instead of speaking the alphabet, those who use American Sign Language (ASL) sign it with their hands. The hand shape and motion for each letter is distinct. For instance, to sign the letter "A," move your hand forward and form the letter "A" shape.

Learning numbers is a crucial part of learning sign language. The hand shapes and movements used to sign the numbers differ from those used to sign the letters of the alphabet. One finger is used to sign the number "1" and five fingers are used to sign the number "5", for instance.

Another crucial component of sign language is facial expression. They can represent a variety of emotions, including joy, sorrow, or confusion. A

88

smile, for instance, can denote happiness whereas a frown, despair.

Additionally, you can study vocabulary words and frequent expressions in sign language. Basic phrases like "hello," "goodbye," "please," and "thank you" can be included in this. You may increase your vocabulary and get a basic command of sign language with practice.

Learning the fundamentals of sign language is enjoyable and helpful. You can begin to communicate with those who are deaf or hard of hearing by learning the alphabet, numbers, facial expressions, and common phrases. Just like learning any other language, mastering sign language requires time and practice, but the work is well worth it.

LEADERSHIP SKILLS:

Understanding the basics of leadership and how to inspire and guide others. The importance of being a positive role model and leader.

Taking responsibility and directing others toward a common objective is what it means to be a leader. Many varied contexts, including school projects, sports teams, and clubs, call for the usage of leadership qualities. Early leadership development is crucial since it will benefit you in the future.

Effective communication is a crucial leadership competency. Effective leaders are able to express their thoughts and objectives to others in a clear manner. They can give clear directions and are able to listen to other people's viewpoints.

Being accountable is a crucial leadership quality. Responsible leaders accept accountability for their own actions as well as those of their team. They ensure that everyone is working toward the same goals and that the work is completed.

Leaders can function well in a collaborative environment. They strive to bring out the best in each team member since they are aware that everyone has unique skills and shortcomings. They also recognize the value of cooperating to accomplish a common objective.

Making decisions is another skill needed for leadership. Good leaders are capable of making choices that are in the group's best interests, even when doing so requires making difficult judgments.

A competent leader should also be able to serve as a positive role model. They set the bar high for others to follow and motivate them to excel. They treat everyone with respect and are trustworthy and honest.

In conclusion, it is critical to develop leadership abilities early in life. You can become a great leader by improving your communication abilities, being accountable, working well in a team, making decisions, and setting a good example. Keep in mind that leadership is a skill that can be developed with time and exposure.

TEAMWORK SKILLS:

Understanding the basics of teamwork, including how to work well with others and achieve shared goals.

The ability to operate as a team to achieve a common objective makes teamwork an essential skill to possess. It is crucial to develop teamwork skills early in life because they will benefit you in many aspects of your life.

Effective communication is one of the key teamwork abilities. Effective team members can articulate their thoughts and opinions to others. They are also receptive to the thoughts and opinions of others and adept at finding points of agreement.

Trust is another critical cooperation competency. Good team members can depend on one other to perform their share and can trust one another. They cooperate with one another since they are aware that everyone has various strengths and weaknesses.

Cooperation is also necessary for teamwork. Effective team members may cooperate and divide the workload. They are aware that teamwork is more productive and efficient than working alone.

Flexibility is another crucial quality. Good team members can adjust to changes and unforeseen circumstances. They are able to adapt since they are aware that plans may occasionally need to be modified.

A good teammate should also be able to show respect. They appreciate one other's viewpoints since they are aware that everyone has a unique perspective. They also recognize that conflicts occur frequently in teams, but they should be able to resolve them amicably.

It is crucial to develop teamwork abilities early in life. You may be a productive team member by developing solid communication skills, trust, cooperation, adaptability, and respect. Keep in mind that teamwork is a talent that can be developed through experience and practice.

Rafiq Khan, MD, PhD

EXERCISE ACTIVITY 8

EXERCISE ACTIVITY 8 "TEAM BUILDING SCAVENGER HUNT"

Objective:

To encourage cooperation, communication, and teamwork among children while having fun.

Materials:

- A list of tasks, pens, and a timer.

Instructions

- Choose a partner to work with.
- Read the list of tasks together and decide who will complete each task.
- Set the timer for 15 minutes and begin working together to complete all the tasks on the list.
- Once the timer goes off, compare the tasks you completed with your partner.
- Reflect on how well you worked together, what challenges you faced, and how you could have improved your teamwork.

- Repeat the activity with different partners to continue practicing teamwork and social skills.
- Task List:
- Draw a picture of a tree together
- Create a story together
- Build a tower using only toothpicks and marshmallows
- Solve a puzzle together
- Group cooking activity

- Come up with a handshake or a cheer that represents your team
- By engaging in this activity, you will learn the importance of cooperation, communication, and teamwork, and practice these skills in a fun and interactive way.

EXERCISE ACTIVITY 9

EXERCISE ACTIVITY 9
"LEADERSHIP SKILLS DEVELOPMENT"

Objective:

To educate children on leadership skills.

Instructions

Task 1: Picture Yourself as a Leader

- Close your eyes and imagine yourself in a leadership role. It could be as the leader of a sports team, a club, a school project, or any other situation you can think of. Describe what you see and feel in this role.

Task 2: Identifying Your Leadership Qualities

- Think about your strengths and what makes you a good leader. Make a list of the qualities you believe you possess that would help you be a successful leader.

Task 3: Role-Playing a Leadership Situation

- Act out a situation where you have to be a leader. It could be resolving a conflict between friends, making a group decision, or any other scenario you can think of. Reflect on how you handled the situation and what you learned from the experience.

Task 4: Making a Plan for Improving Your Leadership Skills

- Think about what you can do to improve your leadership skills. Create a plan for how you can work on developing these skills, such as taking on leadership roles, seeking feedback from others, or practicing effective communication.

Task 5: Reflecting on Your Progress

- Reflect on your progress and the things you have learned about yourself as a leader. Think about what you want to continue working on and what your goals are for the future. Continue developing your leadership skills and look for opportunities to put your skills into practice.

CHAPTER 5.

EDUCATION AND LEARNING

Literacy, math, science, history, geography, technology, creative expression, and study skills.

Growing up involves learning, which is crucial. It aids in our education, the acquisition of new abilities, and personal improvement. The process of learning knowledge, skills, values, beliefs, and habits is known as education. The value of education and learning must be understood from a young age.

Through education, we get the chance to discover new things. Science, math, history, and language arts are just a few of the topics we can investigate. We may learn about our surroundings and how they function through education.

You can improve your critical thinking abilities through learning. It enables you to study data, draw connections, and reach wise judgments. This is a crucial ability to possess since it enables us to get around in the world and make wise decisions.

Education also aids in the growth of our imagination and creativity. It enables us to think creatively and generate original concepts and solutions. Being able to think and solve issues creatively is a key life skill.

Our ability to control ourselves and be self-motivated grows as a result of learning. Setting objectives, working hard to achieve them, and accepting responsibility for our actions are all aided by this.

Learning and education are critical components of development. It enables us to learn new things, acquire new abilities, and improve ourselves. Understanding the value of education and learning at a young age is crucial because it will enable you to successfully navigate the world and make wise decisions. Never forget that learning is a lifetime endeavor and that the time to begin is always now.

HISTORY:

Basic knowledge of world history, including major events and historical figures.

The study of historical occurrences that shaped our world is known as history. It aids in our comprehension of how the world has evolved over time and how it came to be the one we inhabit now. Learning about history is crucial because it aids in our comprehension of the past and how it has influenced the present.

History is broken down into various eras, including ancient, medieval, and modern history. Understanding these various eras helps us comprehend how various cultures and civilizations evolved over time.

We can learn about significant historical personalities and occasions. The world in which we now live has been influenced by these people and events.

We can better grasp how various cultures have interacted with and affected one another by studying history. It aids in our understanding of the genesis of many rites, rituals, and faiths.

History also enables us to comprehend how science and technology have developed and affected our civilization. Remember that history is about the people and events that have shaped our world, not just the dates and names.

GEOGRAPHY:

Basic knowledge of world geography, including major physical and political features.

Geography is the study of the Earth's surface, as well as the creatures and organisms that call it home. It aids in our understanding of the environment we live in, both the geographical elements that are natural and the ways that humans have altered it. Because it enables us to comprehend how the globe is interconnected and how various locations are related to one another, geography is vital to understand.

Geography enables us to comprehend the various facets of the Earth's surface, including its mountains, rivers, oceans, and deserts. We can learn about the many types of landforms, the climatic conditions, and the local flora and fauna, as well as how these factors are affected by location.

Human geography, or the study of how people interact with their environment, is another subject we can research. Farming, construction, and other human activities provide us with information about how the land has been altered. We can discover more about the lifestyles of individuals in other locations as well as the variations in their cultures and economies.

Geography also enables us to comprehend how trade, travel, and communication connect the world. We can discover the various modes of transnational movement of people, things, and ideas, as well as how these have evolved over time.

Finally, geography enlightens us on the value of protecting the environment and its contribution to sustainable development.

Geography is a fascinating and significant subject that aids in our understanding of the world around us. It aids in our comprehension of the Earth's natural features, human impact on them, and the interconnectedness of all things. We may better comprehend our position in the world and how we are connected to other people and places by studying about geography. Keep in mind that geography is not just about facts and maps; it is also about the globe and its inhabitants.

SCIENCE:

Basic scientific concepts and principles, including biology, chemistry, and physics.

Science is the study of the environment we live in. It aids in our comprehension of how things operate and how everything is related. Science education is crucial because it gives us a better understanding of the world and how to improve it.

There are several subfields of science, including physics, chemistry, and biology. Each branch aids in our comprehension of a distinct feature of the natural world. For instance, biology aids in our understanding of living creatures and their interactions with one another, chemistry aids in our understanding of the interactions between various substances, and physics aids in our understanding of how the world functions.

We can also learn about several scientific ideas, like forces, matter, and energy. These ideas aid in our comprehension of how the world operates and how research might improve our quality of life.

Science also teaches us how to improve the world and save the environment. We can discover new approaches to resource preservation, pollution abatement, and endangered species protection.

In conclusion, science is a fascinating and significant subject that aids in our understanding of the world. It aids in our comprehension of how things operate and how everything is related. By studying about science, we can improve our knowledge of the natural world and how to improve it. Remember that science is about understanding and improving the world around us, not just about facts and formulae.

MATH:

Basic mathematical concepts and skills, including numbers, operations, geometry, and measurement.

The study of numbers, forms, and patterns is known as math. It aids in problem-solving and aids in our understanding of how the world around us operates. Learning math is crucial because it fosters logical thought and a quantitative understanding of the world.

It is crucial to learn a variety of fundamental mathematical ideas. Addition, subtraction, multiplication, and division are a few of these ideas. These ideas aid in our comprehension of how to manipulate numbers and address issues.

Additionally, we study fundamental geometry ideas like points, lines, and forms. Geometry teaches us how to measure, compare, and understand how various forms and figures relate to one another.

Fractions are a crucial mathematics topic. Fractions give us insight into how to deal with the components of a whole. We are taught how to multiply, divide, add, subtract, and convert fractions to decimals.

Additionally, we study measurement and how to use various length units, including inches, feet, and meters. This clarifies the measurement of length, weight, and volume.

In conclusion, math is a crucial topic that aids in our understanding of the world. It assists us in developing logical reasoning and a quantitative understanding of the universe. We can better comprehend numbers, shapes, and patterns by learning arithmetic, and we may utilize that understanding to address issues in our daily lives. Keep in mind that math is about more than simply numbers and formulas; it is about having a rational, quantitative perspective of the world.

LITERACY:

Basic reading and writing skills, including phonics and grammar.

We utilize reading and writing on a daily basis, thus they are crucial abilities. They aid in our ability to communicate and comprehend our surroundings. Learning to read and write is crucial because it enables us to communicate clearly with others, express our thoughts and ideas, and understand the material we come across.

One of the most crucial things we do is learn to read. The alphabet and word-sounding techniques are the first things we learn. With age, we develop the ability to comprehend phrases and paragraphs as well as the ability to decipher the meaning of what we read.

Another crucial talent we learn as we mature is writing. We learn how to form words and letters into sentences and paragraphs as well as how to put them together. Writing enables us to share our thoughts and ideas to others.

We can better grasp the world around us by reading and writing. While writing enables us to express ourselves and share our views with others, reading helps us learn new facts and concepts.

Grammar, punctuation, and spelling are all skills we acquire through reading and writing. These are crucial for facilitating efficient communication with others.

We utilize reading and writing on a daily basis, thus they are critical abilities. They assist us in comprehending and expressing the world around us. We develop the capacity to comprehend information and communicate our thoughts and ideas by learning to read and write. To improve your reading and writing, do not forget to practice them frequently.

TECHNOLOGY:

Basic understanding and use of technology, including computers and the internet.

From the computers in our classrooms to the cellphones in our pockets, technology is all around us. We can learn new things, communicate with others, and simplify our lives thanks to technology. It is critical to comprehend how technology operates and practice responsible usage.

There are many various types of technology, including computers, cellphones, tablets, and televisions. These gadgets are used by us to play games, obtain information, and connect with friends and family. In our schools, where we are taught how to utilize computers, the internet, and other digital tools, we also make use of technology.

Other ways that technology benefits us include ensuring our safety, assisting with problem-solving, and facilitating daily activities. For instance, GPS technology aids us in locating our location when we become lost, and medical technology aids in the diagnosis and treatment of ailments by doctors.

But it is crucial to use technology wisely and be conscious of any risks. This include avoiding online information sharing and excessive screen time. It also entails knowing how to validate the information we discover online and being aware of the ways in which technology can be used to promote false information.

In conclusion, technology is a big part of our life and is present everywhere. It makes our life simpler, more socially engaging, and educational. However, it is crucial to know how to safely utilize technology and be aware of the risks. Let us keep in mind to use technology safely and responsibly as we continue to explore it.

CREATIVE EXPRESSION:

Understanding and expressing oneself creatively through art, music, or other forms of self-expression.

Utilizing your imagination to produce something original is the essence of creative expression. It could be anything, such as creating a sculpture or writing a tale. It may be a lot of pleasure to express ourselves creatively since it allows us to let our thoughts and feelings run free.

There are many other ways to express oneself creatively, including through literature, music, dance, and painting. It is a terrific way to express ourselves and a way to display our thoughts and feelings. It may be a terrific way to study as well as a means to discover new things.

We are not afraid to make mistakes when we are being creative. We simply let our imaginations wander and see where they lead. It is a means for us to express all of our emotions, including happiness, sadness, and even rage.

Another excellent way to learn and experiment with new concepts is to create something new. When we create, we use our intellect and creativity to discover new information, resolve issues, and express ourselves.

In conclusion, using our imagination and expressing ourselves through the arts is amazing. It can come in a variety of shapes and can be a lot of fun. We use our creativity to discover new concepts and gain knowledge whether we are creating a picture, a tale, or a sculpture. Remember to allow your creativity run free and to enjoy the process rather than being frightened to make mistakes.

STUDY SKILLS:

Understanding the importance of effective study habits, note-taking, and test-taking strategies.

Being a student entails having a ton to study and remember. But fear not; with effective study techniques, we can make it simpler to comprehend and recall what we learn in class. We can learn more successfully and quickly with the aid of study techniques.

Organization is a key study skill. In order to find what we need when we need it, this entails keeping our school supplies, notes, and assignments organized. The ability to manage your time is a crucial study skill. This entails planning ahead and adhering to it so that we may make sure we have adequate time to study, play, and engage in other activities.

Having the ability to focus when studying is essential. This entails maintaining our attention while working without being sidetracked. Finding a quiet spot to study and eliminating distractions like music or TV will help us focus better.

Active reading is a crucial study ability. This entails engaging in active learning rather than merely reading. Making connections between what we currently know and new knowledge entails asking questions and highlighting pertinent information.

It is critical to practice and review what we have learned. This entails examining our notes and the material we acquired in class so that it will be simpler to recall it on the day of the test or quiz.

In conclusion, effective study techniques are necessary for academic achievement. We may make studying more enjoyable and less stressful by being well-organized, managing our time wisely, concentrating on our studies, actively reading, and revising what we learn. Put these study techniques to use, and you will be well on your road to graduating from college.

EXERCISE ACTIVITY 10

EXERCISE ACTIVITY 10 "IMPROVE READING AND WRITING SKILLS"

Objective:

To educate children on improving their reading and writing skills.

Instructions

Let us work on improving your reading and writing skills together! Here is a fun exercise:

Pick a favorite storybook of yours and read it. As you read, try to identify new vocabulary words.

Write down five words from the story that you do not know the meaning of. Look up the definitions of those words in a dictionary or on the internet.

Write a sentence using each of the five words in your own words.

Share your sentences with a family member or friend and ask them to guess the word based on your sentence.

Read a new storybook and repeat the process.

By doing this exercise, you will be exposed to new words, improve your vocabulary, and practice your writing skills. Have fun!

Chapter 6.

Life Skills

basic home repairs, basic gardening, basic vehicle maintenance, basic cooking, basic sewing, basic photography, basic music, basic art, basic sign language, basic carpentry, basic mechanics.

As we grow older, we will be expected to do more things on our own. Life skills are the abilities that help us take care of ourselves and our families. They are the tools that will help us become independent.

Developing fundamental life skills is crucial because it promotes independence. We will be able to navigate life with more assurance if we learn how to take care of ourselves, cook, manage our money, manage our time, and successfully communicate. Always remember to put these abilities to use and develop them, and you will be well on your way to leading a fulfilling and independent life.

Basic Self-Defense:

Understanding the basics of self-defense and how to stay safe in dangerous situations.

Self-defense is the ability to protect oneself from harm or danger. It is important to learn basic self-defense skills to stay safe and confident in any situation. Here are some tips for basic self-defense:

Know your surroundings: Always pay attention to your environment, who is around you, and what is happening. This will help you react quickly if you feel threatened.

Trust your instincts: If you feel uncomfortable or unsafe, listen to your instincts and leave the situation immediately.

Speak up: If someone is making you feel uncomfortable, say "No" or "Stop" in a loud and clear voice. This can show the person that you mean business and may cause them to back off.

Get away: If you are in danger, try to get away as quickly as possible. If you cannot escape, look for a safe place to hide.

Know your body: Learn how to use your body as a weapon. For example, if someone grabs you, use your elbow to strike them. Or, if you are being pushed, use your feet to push back.

Practice self-defense techniques: Take a self-defense class or practice with a trusted friend or family member to improve your skills.

Remember, self-defense is about protecting yourself and not causing harm to others. Always be respectful and avoid physical confrontations whenever possible. If you are ever in a dangerous situation, call for help and try to stay calm. With these basic self-defense skills, you can stay safe and confident in any situation.

BASIC COOKING SKILLS:

Understanding the basics of cooking and nutrition, including food preparation and kitchen safety.

A useful life skill that may be enjoyable and gratifying is cooking. It might not only help you save money, but it can also be a wonderful way to strengthen relationships with loved ones. You may learn about nutrition and the value of a balanced diet by cooking. Below are some fundamental culinary techniques to get you started.

Food safety is the first fundamental cooking skill. This include washing your hands before and after handling food, maintaining a clean kitchen and cooking equipment, and correctly storing food.

Measuring ingredients is another fundamental skill. To make sure that your recipe has the right number of components, use measuring spoons and cups. This is significant since it has an impact on the flavor and consistency of your food.

After that, you will need to learn how to operate simple kitchen appliances like a stove, oven, and microwave. To securely slice fruits and vegetables, you should also learn how to handle a knife.

Following a recipe is another fundamental cooking skill. This entails reading and comprehending the recipe's directions as well as acquiring all the necessary items before beginning to cook.

Finally, it is critical to get knowledge of various cooking techniques, including boiling, frying, baking, and sautéing. You will be able to prepare more dishes and develop your cooking abilities as a result.

In conclusion, learning to cook at a young age is a rewarding and enjoyable life skill. You will be well on your way to producing delectable meals by adhering to food safety guidelines, measuring ingredients, utilizing fundamental kitchen tools, following a recipe, and learning various cooking techniques. Do not forget to practice and enjoy yourself in the kitchen!

BASIC HOME REPAIRS:

Understanding the basics of home repairs, such as changing a lightbulb, unclogging a drain, and basic DIY skills.

Although they may seem difficult, home repairs are not always difficult. With the correct tools and a little knowledge, you can perform a lot of simple house repairs on your own. In order to keep your house in good shape, here are some simple home repairs you can make.

The first simple home improvement is replacing a light bulb. Anyone can complete this straightforward activity. All you require to reach the fixture is a new lightbulb and a ladder or step stool. Before changing the bulb, make sure the fixture is off electricity.

Unclogging a sink or toilet is another easy DIY project. With a plunger, you can quickly and simply solve this common issue. Simply push and pull on the plunger while it is over the toilet or sink drain to clear the obstruction.

The next thing you should learn is how to fix a leaky faucet. To accomplish this, shut off the water supply to the faucet and swap out the washer or O-ring.

Painting a room is yet another simple home improvement. This can be accomplished by first cleaning the walls, protecting the trim and woodwork using painter's tape, and painting the surfaces with a brush or roller.

It is critical to get knowledge of fundamental home maintenance procedures, including monitoring and replacing the air filters in your Heating, Ventilation, and Air Conditioning (HVAC) system, checking for leaks, and maintaining a clean and tidy home.

Home repairs do not have to be challenging or expensive. You can handle many simple house repairs yourself if you have the necessary tools and a little bit of knowledge. You may maintain your home by changing lightbulbs, cleaning out toilets and sinks, repairing leaking faucets, painting rooms, and completing other simple home maintenance tasks. Always be cautious and request assistance when necessary.

BASIC GARDENING:

Understanding the basics of gardening, including planting, watering, and caring for plants.

Everyone of any age can enjoy gardening as a rewarding and enjoyable activity. It is a fantastic way to get in touch with nature and cultivate your own flowers, fruits, and vegetables. Here is some fundamental gardening advice to get you started.

Choosing a spot for your garden is the first step in gardening. This area has to have good soil drainage and receive lots of sunlight.

The soil must then be prepared by getting rid of any weeds and adding organic material, such as compost or manure. This will assist in retaining moisture in the soil and supplying nutrients to the plants.

It is critical to choose plants that are suitable for your region's climate and the amount of sunshine received by your garden. You can either buy seedlings or start your own indoor seedlings from seed.

Additionally, it is crucial to give your plants regular waterings and fertilization on a regular basis. The plants will gain strength and health as a result.

Pest control is a key component of gardening. You can employ a variety of natural pest management techniques, such as companion planting or making your own insecticide, to get rid of pests.

It is critical to correctly care for your fruits, veggies, and flowers as well as to harvest them at the appropriate time.

People of all ages can enjoy gardening, which is a rewarding and enjoyable hobby. You may cultivate your own garden by picking the ideal place, preparing the soil, selecting the perfect plants, routinely watering and fertilizing, managing pests, and harvesting and caring for your fruits, veggies, and flowers. Always be cautious and request assistance when necessary.

BASIC SEWING:

Understanding the basics of sewing, including how to use a sewing machine and basic stitching techniques.

You may make your own clothes, accessories, and home decor by learning to sew. Sewing is enjoyable and practical. You will discover some fundamental sewing skills in this post that will aid you in beginning your sewing journey.

Threading the needle is the first step in sewing. You will require a needle, thread, and a pair of scissors to do this. Cut a piece of thread that is about the length of your arm to begin. After that, thread the needle by inserting the thread into the needle's eye.

After that, you will discover how to knot the thread's end. As you sew, this will prevent your thread from unraveling.

At the end of the thread, create a tiny loop, and then knot it on top of the loop.

Another fundamental sewing technique that is essential is the running stitch. Two pieces of cloth are joined with a running stitch, which is a simple back-and-forth stitch. Run the needle through the fabric on one side, then through the opposite side, and repeat to make a running stitch.

You ought to master whipstitching as well. A whipstitch is a stitch that joins two pieces of fabric together or is used as an edge finisher.

To create a whipstitch, pass the needle through the fabric twice: once through one side and once through the other.

Finally, you should become proficient at sewing buttons and snap closures. Snap fasteners can be fastened by using a special tool to press the snap fastener into the cloth, as opposed to buttons, which can be stitched on by creating a loop of thread and attaching it to the fabric with a button.

You may make your own clothes, accessories, and home decor by learning to sew. Sewing is enjoyable and practical. You can make your own patterns and projects by learning fundamental sewing skills including how to thread a needle, tie a knot, create a running stitch, whipstitch, and attach buttons or snap fasteners. Always exercise patience and keep practicing!

EXERCISE ACTIVITY 11

EXERCISE ACTIVITY 11
"ACTIVITY TO LEARN SELF-DEFENSE"

Objective:

To educate children on self-defense.

Instructions

In today's world, it is essential to have the skills to protect yourself and stay safe in different situations.

Let us work together to develop your self-defense abilities.

Begin by standing tall with confidence. Keep your chin up and your shoulders back.

Next, work on your stance. Stand with your feet hip-width apart, and have your knees slightly bent.

Now, practice blocking. Imagine someone coming towards you and use your arms to block the attack.

Finally, work on striking. Imagine punching or kicking the attacker while using the correct technique.

Practice these steps several times and make sure to keep practicing every day.

Self-defense involves not only physical strength but also being aware of your surroundings and having confidence in your abilities.

Keep up the great work!

CHAPTER 7.

CAREER AND PROFESSIONAL DEVELOPMENT

Career exploration, entrepreneurship, civic engagement, public speaking, mental math, negotiation skills, project management, research skills, self-reflection, self-motivation, digital literacy, and data analysis.

Growing up and making plans for the future involve many key aspects, including career and professional development. Finding and preparing for the type of employment you want to do when you are older is the process of career development. Professional development is the process of acquiring knowledge and new abilities that will help you succeed in your chosen field of work.

There are numerous professions to choose from, like those of a doctor, educator, scientist, engineer, artist, or musician, to name a few. While some people may be unsure of their career goals as they become older, others may be certain. It is crucial to research various professions and identify your hobbies.

It is crucial to perform well in school and gain as much knowledge as you can in order to prepare for a profession. This will provide you a strong foundation and enable you to succeed in any field you decide to pursue. Participating in extracurricular activities like clubs, athletics, and volunteer work is crucial as well. You can learn valuable skills from these activities, like communication, leadership, and teamwork.

As you get older, you might want to consider volunteering or taking up a part-time job to obtain experience. This will assist you in learning more about various vocations and acquiring significant abilities that will be beneficial in your future employment.

For your job, professional development is equally crucial. This entails picking up knowledge and developing new abilities that will help you succeed in your chosen field of work. This can involve enrolling in classes, going to seminars or workshops, or taking part in mentorship programs.

You will carry on learning and developing as a person as you age. You might change your mind about what you want to accomplish for a job as well as your hobbies and skills. That is alright! It is crucial to be receptive to new possibilities and eager to learn and develop.

In summary, career and professional development are crucial components of maturing and making plans for the future. It is crucial to investigate several job options, perform well in school, and acquire work experience. Professional development is crucial for maintaining personal growth and learning. You may attain your professional goals and have a fulfilling job with the correct attitude, abilities, and knowledge.

CAREER EXPLORATION:

Understanding the basics of different career options and how to research and explore different career paths

It is crucial to start looking into numerous employment options as you become older and start considering your future. It can be difficult to select the ideal employment for you because there are so many different jobs available. It is crucial to start considering other jobs while you are still young because of this.

Talking to people who work in various fields is one approach to investigate several career options. You might enquire about their jobs and find out what they enjoy and dislike about them. To find out more about various jobs and the education and training needed for them, you can also conduct research online.

Try out several interests and pastimes as a method to explore various careers. For instance, you might be interested in a job in carpentry or mechanics if you like working with your hands. A job in math or finance may be of interest to you if you enjoy working with numbers.

It is crucial to consider what you value in a work. Do you want to work in a team, or do you desire a job that allows you to be independent? Do you prefer to work with tools or technology, or do you desire a career where you can assist others?

Keep in mind that it is never too early to start considering your options for a profession.

Your ability to decide on your future will improve as you get more knowledge about various careers.

It is also critical to consider your interests and passions, as well as what you value in a career. This will assist you in locating a profession that you will find enjoyable and fulfilling.

Career exploration, in its simplest form, is the process of determining what kind of job you would enjoy doing in the future by learning about various professions, speaking with people who hold those positions, and trying out various extracurricular activities and hobbies. In order to be able to make judgments about your future, it is crucial to begin considering jobs when you are still young.

SELF-MOTIVATION SKILLS:

Understanding the basics of self-motivation and how to set and achieve goals.

Self-motivation is a vital talent that can support your success in life and enable you to accomplish your goals. You need to push yourself to perform at your highest level and realize your entire potential.

Setting objectives for yourself is a good method to increase self-motivation. Consider your goals, such as improving your grades, meeting new people, or participating in a sport. Make a strategy for achieving your goals after you have set them. Set deadlines for yourself and list the steps you must take.

Keeping a positive outlook is another way to promote self-motivation. Have confidence in your skills and abilities. Do not give up when you run into problems or barriers. Instead, consider how to get around them. Spend time with supportive and motivating people.

Additionally, it is critical to accept accountability for your deeds. Do not point the finger to others if something goes wrong. Instead, spend some time

ESSENTIAL LIFE SKILLS FOR YOUTH

considering what you may have done better and how you can improve moving forward.

Finally, remember to look after yourself. Eat well, get adequate rest, and work out frequently. Physical well-being makes it simpler to feel motivated.

In conclusion, the ability to be self-motivated can help you realize your potential and fulfill your goals. Set goals for yourself, have a positive outlook, own up to your mistakes, surround yourself with encouraging people, and look after yourself. You may cultivate self-motivation and become a successful person with time and effort.

BASIC DIGITAL LITERACY:

Understanding the basics of digital literacy and how to use technology safely and responsibly

Digital literacy is the capacity to use technology for information creation, evaluation, and communication. In the modern world, when technology is incorporated into many facets of our everyday life, it is a crucial talent to possess.

Basic computer literacy abilities include:

Using the mouse and keyboard, running and stopping applications, and being familiar with a computer's basic architecture are all part of learning how to use a computer.

Understanding the internet includes things like knowing how to use a web browser to access websites, how to utilize search engines, and how to stay safe online.

Using email: This entails knowing how to accomplish both sending and receiving emails, as well as how to act appropriately and respectfully while doing so.

Using social media: This entails being aware of how to act responsibly and safely on platforms like Facebook, Instagram, and TikTok.

Digital content creation includes using apps like Microsoft Word and Google Docs to produce documents, taking photos and videos with a camera or smartphone, and editing them using simple editing tools.

You will be better equipped to navigate the digital world and use technology to communicate, learn, and create in a secure and responsible way if you acquire these fundamental digital literacy abilities.

Basic Presentation Skills:

Understanding the basics of presentation skills, including how to effectively communicate information to an audience.

Effective audience communication requires the capacity to effectively convey ideas and information. They are crucial for a variety of situations in life, including giving a speech, presenting a class project, or simply just explaining something to a buddy.

Some fundamental presentation abilities include:

Knowing your subject well, arranging your data, and putting up a visual aid to assist you clarify your points, such as a slide presentation or poster, are all examples of preparation.

Making eye contact with your audience, speaking clearly and loudly enough for everyone to hear, and utilizing suitable body language are all examples of confidence.

Keeping your audience engaged and involved in your presentation requires engaging them. This includes sharing tales, asking questions, and using visual aids.

Being adaptable means being able to change your presentation depending on the audience and being ready to respond to queries and resolve issues that might arise.

In order to feel more at ease and confident when presenting your presentation, you should practice it in front of friends, family, or even a mirror.

You will be able to effectively communicate your ideas and facts to an audience in a clear, confident, and entertaining way by acquiring these fundamental presentation skills.

SELF-REFLECTION SKILLS:

Understanding the basics of self-reflection and how to evaluate and improve oneself.

Self-reflection is a crucial talent that can aid in self-understanding and the implementation of life-improving adjustments. It entails reflecting on our aims and objectives as they connect to our ideas, feelings, and behavior.

Setting aside time each day to reflect on your experiences is one method to develop self-reflection. You can accomplish this by keeping a journal, speaking with a dependable friend or relative, or even just sitting quietly and reflecting.

Consider both what you did well and what you could have done differently as you reflect. Consider your feelings and the lessons you might draw from them. And think about what you want to do the following time you encounter a similar circumstance.

Thinking about your objectives and values is another exercise in self-reflection. What goals do you have for your life? What matters most to you? Which personality type do you wish to be? You may make decisions that are in line with your objectives and values by giving these questions some thought.

You can find patterns in your conduct that might be limiting you by reflecting on your own actions. Consider why you might procrastinate frequently, for instance, and what you might do to improve it.

In conclusion, self-reflection is a potent tool that can aid in self-understanding, life-improving changes, and goal achievement. You can develop your capacity for self-reflection and maximize your potential by making time for contemplation, reflecting on your past experiences, setting objectives, and considering your beliefs.

PROJECT MANAGEMENT SKILLS:

Understanding the basics of project management, including how to plan, organize and execute projects successfully.

A task or series of tasks that you must finish make up a project. The process of organizing, managing, and supervising a project from beginning to end is known as project management. Basic project management abilities are crucial since they enable you to stay on schedule and organized when working on a project.

Setting objectives and putting together a plan are crucial when managing a project. Making a list of the tasks that must be done and figuring out when and how to execute each one is part of this process. Keeping track of your work will help you determine whether you are on pace to complete the job by the deadline.

Communication is a crucial component of project management. You must be able to articulate your strategy and objectives to others, as well as request assistance or resources as needed.

It is critical to be adaptable and receptive to change. When things do not go according to plan, you may need to modify your plan. The ability to adjust and change course when necessary is a crucial component of project management.

Simply said, fundamental project management abilities include goal setting, planning, monitoring progress, effective communication, and being adaptable and open to change. You can successfully and effectively finish undertakings with the help of these abilities.

ENTREPRENEURSHIP:

Understanding the basics of starting and running a business.

The process of creating and operating your own business is referred to as entrepreneurship. Making your ideas into reality and changing the world is exhilarating and difficult at the same time.

Being an entrepreneur requires being imaginative, resourceful, and risk-taking. You must be able to generate fresh ideas and transform them into company plans. This entails finding out about your industry, your target market, your competitors, and what it takes to succeed in company.

Good communication skills are also necessary for entrepreneurship. You must be able to articulate your ideas to people and convince them to support your venture or purchase your goods. Additionally, you must be able to get along with others, whether they are clients, partners, or coworkers.

Entrepreneurs must also be adept at making decisions and addressing problems. Starting a business is difficult, and there will be many obstacles to overcome. You must possess the capacity for quick decision-making and on-the-spot thinking.

Strong work ethics are also a requirement for entrepreneurs. It takes a lot of effort and commitment to launch a business. To build a successful business, you will need to put in a lot of work and sacrifice.

In conclusion, entrepreneurship is a difficult yet rewarding career path that can help you realize your ideas and change the world. It necessitates imagination, inventiveness, effective communication and problem-solving abilities, a solid work ethic, and the willingness to take chances.

PUBLIC SPEAKING:

Understanding the basics of public speaking, including effective communication and body language.

Being able to communicate your thoughts and ideas to people clearly and successfully through public speaking is a crucial ability to have. Speaking in front of a group of people might be intimidating, but with practice, it can become less intimidating and even pleasurable.

Participating in presentations and conversations in class is one method to begin developing your public speaking skills. Despite your anxiety, speak out and share your thoughts. Joining a club or group that specializes on public speaking, such a debate club or a theater group, is another option to practice.

It is crucial to thoroughly understand your content when getting ready for a public speaking event. Several times before the occasion, practice your speech or presentation. Make sure you speak clearly and loudly and keep your pace consistent. To better communicate your message, use gestures and facial expressions.

The use of body language is a crucial component of public speaking. Use your hands to highlight points, stand up straight, and look the audience in the eye. To convey that you are at ease speaking in front of others, use open, resolute body language.

Finally, it is critical to maintain composure and ease when speaking in front of a crowd. Breathe deeply and keep in mind that making mistakes is acceptable. You will feel more at ease and confident as you practice public speaking.

In conclusion, practicing and gaining experience will help you improve your public speaking abilities. At first, it could be unsettling, but with practice, you will gain confidence and improve your communication skills. You will succeed if you practice, project confidence through your body language, and maintain composure.

NEGOTIATION SKILLS:

Understanding the basics of negotiation, including how to communicate effectively and reach mutually beneficial agreements.

Your ability to negotiate can help you achieve your goals in life. It involves talking with someone and coming to a mutually beneficial solution in order to come to an agreement. You can use negotiation as a helpful tool to improve many aspects of your life, like working out a timetable for doing chores with your brother and obtaining a higher allowance from your parents.

Here are some pointers for the fundamentals of negotiation:

Know what you want: Be certain that you are clear on your goals before engaging in any negotiations. You will be able to focus better and avoid becoming distracted if you do this.

Actively listen: Pay close attention to the other person's perspective and make an effort to comprehend where they are coming from. This will enable you to establish rapport and cooperate on a solution.

Respect others: Treat them with courtesy and refrain from using foul words or raising your voice. When both parties in a negotiation feel heard and appreciated, the chances of a good outcome increase.

Be adaptable: Be receptive to alternative approaches and prepared to make concessions. Even while you might not always be able to acquire exactly what you want, you can still come to a compromise that benefits you.

Be assured: When bargaining, speak simply and with assurance. By doing this, you will be able to convince the other individual that you're serious and confident in your arguments.

In conclusion, developing effective negotiation techniques is a life skill that should begin as soon as possible. You can acquire the abilities required to become a skilled negotiator and obtain what you want in life with practice and perseverance.

NETWORKING SKILLS:

Understanding the basics of networking and how to connect with others.

Everyone should have networking abilities. The main goal of networking is to establish connections and rapport with people. You can make acquaintances, network, and seize opportunities thanks to it.

Here are some pointers for fostering networking abilities at an early age:

Be welcoming and receptive: Approach anyone you meet for the first time with a grin and a happy disposition. They will be more inclined to approach you after hearing this.

Pose inquiries: Ask the person you are speaking with questions about yourself. This keeps the conversation continuing and demonstrates your interest in learning more about them.

Actively listen: Make sure you comprehend what the other person is saying and pay close attention to what they are saying. This will enable you to establish a stronger bond with them.

Be useful: Make an offer to assist someone if you can. This will demonstrate your concern for them and may encourage them to assist you in return.

Following up: Make sure to get in touch with anyone you meet later if you think they are intriguing. You might do this by sending them an email or scheduling another meeting.

Keep in mind that networking requires time and practice. You will get better at it the more you practice. So, continue making new friends and developing connections. In the long term, it will be beneficial!

BASIC RESEARCH SKILLS:

Understanding the basics of research, including how to gather and analyze information effectively.

A valuable skill that can benefit you in many aspects of life is the ability to conduct research. You can utilize research to learn more about a subject by gathering data and improving your understanding of it. When you are attempting to decide or solve a problem, research skills are very helpful.

To do research, you must be aware of your study objectives before you can begin. You might begin by compiling a list of the inquiries you wish to pursue. Next, a range of resources, including books, internet, and databases, can be used to find information. It is critical to be selective about the sources you use and to confirm the veracity and accuracy of the data you uncover.

When you have located the information, organize and analyze it. You can take notes, underline critical material, and divide information into categories. This will make it easier for you to comprehend the data and make connections between various bits of information.

It is crucial to share what you have learnt, to finish. You might show your findings to others or create a report outlining them. This will both help you grasp the subject more clearly and allow others to benefit from your research.

You can explore new subjects and ideas and have a better grasp of the world around you by honing your research abilities. So, stay at it and never stop being curious!

BASIC DATA ANALYSIS:

Understanding the basics of data analysis and how to analyze and interpret data effectively.

Data analysis is an important skill that helps us understand and make sense of information. Just like how we use addition and subtraction to solve math problems, data analysis allows us to look at numbers and data to find answers to questions and make decisions.

A simple way to understand data analysis is to think about collecting and organizing information, like making a chart or graph. For example, if we want to know what our favorite snack is, we can ask our friends and keep track of the results in a chart. Then, we can look at the chart and see which snack is the most popular.

Another example of data analysis is looking at graphs and charts to understand patterns or trends. For example, if we look at a graph of the weather over the past month, we can see if it has been getting warmer or colder.

Learning data analysis can help us in many ways. It can help us make decisions and solve problems in a more efficient and effective way. It can also help us understand information and see patterns that we might not have noticed before.

Overall, data analysis is a valuable skill that is important to learn and can help us in many areas of life. By starting to practice data analysis at a young age, you can become confident and skilled in this area as you grow up.

INTERVIEW SKILLS:

Understanding the basics of interview skills and how to present oneself effectively in an interview.

For anyone, including young people who are just learning how to navigate the world of work and professional advancement, interviews may be nerve-wracking experiences. However, with the correct planning and abilities, interviews can also be a terrific chance to showcase your capabilities and leave a positive first impression. You should be familiar with the following fundamental interview techniques:

Take the time to learn about the organization and the position you are applying for before the interview. This will assist you understand what the interviewer is looking for and enable you to customize your responses to the needs of the business.

Think about the frequent inquiries that are posed during interviews and rehearse your responses. You will feel more assured and prepared to respond to any queries the interviewer may have as a result.

First impressions are important, so make sure you are properly attired for the interview. Pick out clean, organized, and comfortable clothing.

Be respectful and courteous. Throughout the interview, use appropriate demeanor and be courteous to the interviewer. This includes making eye contact, asking politely, and expressing thank you.

Be genuine. Being genuine is crucial throughout the interview. Be upfront and truthful when describing your background, passions, and abilities. This will enable the interviewer to learn more about you and assess whether you are a good fit for the business.

In conclusion, while getting ready for an interview requires time and work, it is ultimately worthwhile. By employing these fundamental interview techniques, you will have the self-assurance to succeed and leave a lasting impression.

RESUME AND COVER LETTER WRITING:

Understanding the basics of resume and cover letter writing and how to effectively market oneself to potential employers.

For job seekers, a resume and cover letter are crucial tools. They introduce themselves to prospective employers and highlight their qualifications. It can be intimidating to write a resume and cover letter, but it is a crucial skill to develop early. Here are some pointers for you who are only now beginning to learn about these important documents.

Your name, address, phone number, and email should all be noted down at the outset.

Write a quick introduction about yourself, mentioning your hobbies, abilities, and future goals.

you would include any jobs, volunteer positions, or extracurricular activities in your list of previous experiences, if any. You would also highlight any accomplishments or talents that are pertinent to the position you are looking for.

The next step would be to write a cover letter. Use the recipient's name if you can when addressing the letter to them in the beginning. Describe your motivations for applying for the position and why you would be a good fit for the organization.

Thank the reader for their time and share your excitement about the chance as you end the cover letter.

Keep in mind that the purpose of your resume and cover letter is to demonstrate that you are an accomplished applicant who would make a valuable contribution to the organization. To make the finest impression, it is crucial to take the time to write them attentively. You may master the art of writing resumes and cover letters with time and effort.

Work-Life Balance:

Understanding the importance of maintaining a healthy balance between work and personal life.

Work-life balance is about striking a balance between the time and energy you put into your work and the time and care you put into the other important aspects of your life, such spending time with family and friends, pursuing hobbies and interests, and taking care of yourself.

You should start learning how to create balance in your life even if you are not working yet. This is because the behaviors you develop now will influence how you will see work-life balance in the future. To get you started, consider these suggestions:

Make a list of your top priorities and sort the list according to priority. You can make sure that your time and effort are being focused on the things that are most crucial by doing this.

Make time for pleasure. Be sure to set aside time each day for the activities you enjoy. This can entail exercising, reading a book, or conversing with friends.

To keep motivated and engaged, take breaks from your work or studies. Try to allot some time each day for stretching, walking, or resting.

Ensure that you get enough sleep every night so that you have the energy to do your responsibilities and enjoy time with your friends.

Do not be hesitant to seek for help if you're feeling overwhelmed. You can seek assistance from a teacher, parent, or friend.

Always keep in mind that finding balance is a process, so it is good if it takes some time to discover what suits you the best. You may live a happy and satisfying life by striking the correct balance between work and recreation with a little effort and the right attitude.

EXERCISE ACTIVITY 12

EXERCISE ACTIVITY 12 "CAREER AND PROFESSIONAL DEVELOPMENT"

Objective:

To educate children on career and professional development.

Instructions

Step 1:

Identify your interests and skills. Take some time to think about what you are good at and what you enjoy doing. Make a list of these things.

Step 2:

Research careers that match your interests and skills. Look up job descriptions, salary ranges, and what kind of education and training is required.

Step 3:

Based on your research, decide on a career goal and create a plan to achieve it. This can include getting a certain education, learning specific skills, or gaining relevant experience.

Step 4:

Start working on your plan by taking classes, volunteering, or seeking out job opportunities in your desired field.

Step 5:

Evaluate your progress and make adjustments. Regularly assess your progress and make changes to your plan as needed.
Good luck on your career journey!

EXERCISE ACTIVITY 13

EXERCISE ACTIVITY 13 "PROJECT MANAGEMENT ACTIVITY"

Objective:

To educate children on project management skills.

Instructions

Step 1:
Choose a project. It could be anything from planning a birthday party to building a birdhouse etc.

Step 2:
Break down the project into smaller tasks. Write each task on a separate index card.

Step 3:
Prioritize the tasks. Decide which tasks need to be done first and which ones can wait.

Step 4:
Create a timeline. Use a calendar or a timeline chart to visualize when each task needs to be completed.

Step 5:
Monitor your progress. Check your timeline and make sure you are staying on track. If you are running behind, see if there is anything you can do to catch up.

Remember, project management skills are important not just for school projects but also for everyday life. By breaking down big tasks into smaller ones and creating a plan, you will be able to accomplish your goals and achieve success!

CHAPTER 8.

PERSONAL FINANCE AND BASIC BUDGETING

Personal finance and budgeting are important skills that everyone needs to learn. Having a good understanding of money and how to manage it can help you achieve your goals and lead a happy and stress-free life.

MONEY MANAGEMENT:

Basic concepts of earning, saving, spending, and budgeting money, as well as understanding the value of money.

Money management is an important skill that everyone should learn. It helps us understand how to manage our money effectively and make smart decisions about how we use it. Here are some basic concepts that you can start to learn about money management:

Saving: It is never too early to start saving money. Set aside money for future goals, such as buying a gadget or saving for college. Save a portion of your allowance or any money you receive as gifts.

Budgeting: Create a budget by setting aside money for necessities like food and clothing, and also allow some money for fun expenses like going to the movies or buying a new book.

Earning money: You can earn money by doing chores or starting your own business, such as selling lemonade. This will help you understand the value of hard work and how it relates to money.

Spending wisely: Understand the difference between needs and wants. You should only spend money on things you need and save up for things you want.

Giving: Understand the importance of giving back to others by donating money to charity or helping others in need. This will help instill a sense of compassion and generosity in you.

By learning these basic concepts, you can start to develop good money management habits that will serve you well throughout your life. It is important to remember that money management is a lifelong process and there is always room for improvement and growth.

PERSONAL FINANCE:

Understanding the basics of personal finance, including budgeting, saving, investing, and credit management.

Personal finance is an important aspect of life that helps people understand how to manage their money and make smart financial decisions. It is never too early to start learning about basic personal finance concepts.

One of the most important personal finance skills is understanding how to save and budget money. This means setting aside a portion of the money you receive, such as allowance or gifts, for things like long-term savings or spending on future plans. It also means being mindful of how you spend money and making smart choices to avoid overspending.

Another important personal finance skill is learning about different types of money, such as cash, checks, debit cards, and credit cards. Knowing the advantages and disadvantages of each type of money can help you make informed decisions about how to spend and save it.

Additionally, it is important for you to understand the importance of setting and reaching financial goals. Whether it is saving up for a big purchase, like a new toy or bike, or setting aside money for the future, having a plan for your money can help you feel in control of your finances.

Finally, it is important to talk to trusted adults, such as parents or teachers, about personal finance questions and concerns. They can offer guidance and support as you learn more about managing your money.

In conclusion, personal finance is an important skill that can help you make smart decisions about money. By learning about saving, budgeting, different types of money, setting financial goals, and talking to trusted adults, you can get a solid foundation in personal finance.

BASIC PERSONAL BUDGETING:

Understanding the basics of personal budgeting and how to manage finances.

You can keep track of your finances and ensure you have enough money to cover all your expenses by using a budget, which is a crucial life skill. Your age is an excellent starting age to learn about budgeting because it is never too early!

Simply put, a budget is an outline of your financial priorities. Knowing how much money comes in and leaves your account each month is necessary to develop a budget. The money you earn through sources including gifts, part-time work, and allowance is referred to as income. Your expenditures include things like food, clothing, toys, and recreational activities.

Making a financial plan for your money can begin once you are aware of your income and expenses. Make a list of all your expenses first, and then calculate how much money is left over after covering all of your basic expenses, including food, clothing, and housing. Choose your next course of action for the remaining funds. Perhaps you would like to keep it or spend it on enjoyable items like hobbies or toys.

Budgets are not fixed in stone, so keep that in mind. You can change your budget by reducing spending in another area if you find that you spent more money than you intended on one item. Making trade-offs is what we refer to as, and it is a crucial step in budgeting.

Keeping track of your spending is one budgeting strategy that might be useful. To achieve this, keep a written record of all your financial transactions, including the items purchased. This will make it easy for you to monitor where your money is going and, if necessary, to change your budget.

Overall, creating a budget is a fantastic method to practice good money management and ensure that you have enough money to pay for all your expenses. You will quickly become an expert at budgeting with a little perseverance and practice.

EXERCISE ACTIVITY 14

EXERCISE ACTIVITY 14
"BUDGETING FOR A MONTH"

Objective:

To educate children on personal finance and budgeting.

Instructions

Step 1:
Gather information - Write down all the sources of income you receive in a month, such as an allowance, gifts, or any part-time jobs. Also, list all the expenses you have for the month, including food, entertainment, transportation, etc.

Step 2:
Create a budget plan - Based on the information gathered in step 1, create a budget plan for the month. Set aside money for necessary expenses, such as food and transportation, and allocate some money for discretionary expenses, such as entertainment or hobbies.

Step 3:
Track expenses - Keep a record of all the money you spend during the month and compare it to your budget plan.

Step 4:
Analyze and adjust - At the end of the month, analyze how closely you followed your budget plan and make any necessary adjustments.

By completing this task, you can learn the importance of budgeting and managing your finances effectively.

CHAPTER 9.

MENTAL HEALTH AND STRESS MANAGEMENT

Understanding the importance of mental health and how to maintain it.

Our total well-being is greatly influenced by our mental health. It influences our daily thoughts, emotions, and behaviors. The same way that our physical health can be impacted by several things including stress, relationships, and life events, so can our mental health.

It is crucial for you to comprehend the fundamentals of mental health and how to take care of it. Here are a few advice:

Self-care can be as basic as getting enough sleep, eating a nutritious diet, and exercising. These routines can improve our general well-being and mood.

Do not be hesitant to express your sentiments and speak to someone you trust, like a parent or a teacher, about how you are feeling. They can assist you in comprehending and managing your emotions.

Learn how to relax. Yoga or a few deep breaths can help you calm down and lower your stress levels.

Be around positive people. Being around individuals who are encouraging and optimistic can have a significant impact on our mental health.

When you feel overwhelmed or depressed, do not be afraid to seek for assistance. Speak with a responsible adult or a mental health specialist.

In summary, maintaining your mental health is just as crucial as maintaining your physical health. You can learn how to create healthy habits and uphold good mental health for the future by employing these straightforward suggestions.

MENTAL AND EMOTIONAL HEALTH:

Understanding the basics of mental and emotional health and how to maintain overall well-being.

We all know how crucial mental and emotional wellness are to our entire wellbeing. Our thoughts and emotions require attention just as much as our physical bodies do to be in good health. You can follow these simple guidelines to preserve good mental and emotional health:

Exercise self-care: It is critical to look after your mental and emotional well-being. You can feel better by engaging in simple activities like getting adequate sleep, eating well, and exercising.

Express your emotions: We occasionally experience emotions that are challenging to comprehend or manage. It is critical to express these emotions and discuss them with someone you can trust. A parent, teacher, or counselor can be this.

Practice mindfulness: Being attentive means being aware of your thoughts and feelings while being present in the moment. Simple mindfulness practices like journaling, deep breathing, and meditation can give you a sense of calmness and control.

Embrace a positive environment: Being around people who **uplift** and inspire you can improve your self-confidence, make you happier, and increase your sense of well-being. Try to spend time with loved ones and people who uplift you.

Manage your stress: Stress is a natural part of life, but too much of it can be bad for your mental and emotional well-being. You can manage stress successfully by using easy stress-reduction tactics like deep breathing, exercise, and taking pauses.

It is never too early to begin caring for your mental and emotional health, so keep that in mind. You will be laying the foundation for a lifetime of happiness and wellbeing by putting these habits into practice.

STRESS MANAGEMENT:

Understanding the basics of stress management and how to effectively manage and reduce stress.

When you are young, it can be challenging to understand what stress is. However, it is crucial to understand that stress is a normal part of life and that everyone experiences it occasionally. Stress can be brought on by a variety of factors, including family issues, professional obligations, and lifestyle changes. The good news is that learning about different stress management techniques can be started early.

Taking care of oneself is one of the most crucial things you can do to handle stress. This includes consuming wholesome foods, obtaining appropriate rest, and engaging in enjoyable physical activity. You can also try to engage in activities that make you joyful, such as socializing with friends, participating in sports, or creating crafts. You can feel better both physically and mentally by carrying out these actions.

Learning how to relax is a crucial component of managing stress. This can entail deep breathing exercises, meditation, or physical exercise like yoga or stretching. You might also try to concentrate on the blessings in your life and try to see obstacles as chances to develop and learn.

It is crucial to express your feelings to someone, especially if you're feeling overwhelmed. A parent, teacher, or close friend can serve in this capacity. They can listen to you and provide encouragement and counsel. Asking for assistance is OK if you ever feel like you cannot manage your stress. There is no shame in doing that, and it is always preferable to seek assistance when you do.

Finally, even though stress is a natural part of life, it is crucial to know how to handle it. You may strengthen your resilience and improve your ability to manage stress by taking care of yourself, finding ways to unwind, talking to someone about your thoughts, and asking for assistance when you need it. It is never too early to begin learning stress management techniques, and maintaining good mental and emotional health is crucial for leading a happy and full life.

MENTAL MATH:

Understanding the basics of mental math and how to perform calculations quickly.

The capacity to conduct mathematical calculations mentally, without the use of a calculator or paper, is known as mental math. It is a practical ability that facilitates quick and effective problem-solving and can enhance your general mathematical abilities.

Simple addition, subtraction, multiplication, and division problems can be used to use your mind to solve problems. Regular practice is crucial, as is the use of visual aids to assist with the computations, such as number lines or grouping things. As you advance, you can try resolving more challenging issues and even attempting to use mental math while carrying out other tasks, like playing a sport or preparing food.

Focusing on mastering arithmetic facts, such as the multiplication tables, will help you remember them quickly in the future. Mental math can also be made simpler by comprehending the underlying ideas, such as place value and estimation.

Additionally, it is critical to have patience with yourself and maintain your composure when you make mistakes. You can improve your confidence and skill in your capacity to make calculations in your head with practice, time, and effort.

It is important to keep in mind that mental math is a useful skill that can be used to many facets of life, including shopping, cooking, and problem-solving. So, continue to practice and enjoy it!

MENTAL AND PHYSICAL HEALTH:

Understanding the link between physical and mental health and how to maintain both.

Both physical and mental health are crucial components of our total well-being. Our minds require adequate care and attention just like our bodies do to remain healthy and powerful.

Our physical condition, which includes our body's capacity to move, develop, and react to various stimuli, is referred to as our physical health. Regular exercise, wholesome nutrition, and adequate rest are all ways we can maintain our physical health.

On the other side, mental health is a term that describes our emotional, psychological, and social well-being. It influences our daily thoughts, emotions, and actions. Taking care of our emotions, controlling our stress levels, and developing close relationships with those around us are all important components of maintaining our mental health.

It is critical to keep in mind that mental and physical health are intertwined, with one potentially having an impact on the other. For instance, stress or anxiety might affect our physical health by resulting in headaches, muscle strain, or sleep issues.

Similar to how feeling physically unwell can affect our mental health, feeling unwell can also make us frustrated, depressed, or anxious.

Mental and physical health are closely linked and have a big impact on each other. When our mind is healthy and happy, it can help our body feel better too. On the other hand, when we are feeling sad, anxious, or stressed, our body can feel tired, achy, and even get sick.

For example, if we exercise regularly, it can help us feel happy and relaxed. Exercise releases endorphins, which are chemicals in our brain that make us feel good. Regular exercise can also help improve our physical health by making our muscles stronger, our hearts healthier, and our bodies more flexible.

Similarly, eating healthy foods, getting enough sleep, and taking care of ourselves also helps us feel good both mentally and physically. On the other hand, skipping meals, staying up late, or neglecting our health can make us feel tired, unhappy, and even sick.

It is important to understand the link between mental and physical health and to make sure we are taking care of both. This can help us feel our best and be ready to tackle whatever challenges come our way. Whether it is playing outside with friends, trying new hobbies, or simply taking a deep breath and counting to ten, there are many ways to take care of both our mental and physical health.

EXERCISE ACTIVITY 15

EXERCISE ACTIVITY 15
"STRESS MANAGEMENT ACTIVITY"

Objective:

To educate children on stress management skills.

Instructions

Step 1: Identify your stress triggers

Think about what usually causes you to feel stressed. It could be things like school, family problems, or even just having too much to do. Write down a list of these stress triggers.

Step 2: Brainstorm stress-management techniques

Do some research or think about what helps you feel calm and relaxed. Some examples might include deep breathing, exercise, or spending time with friends. Write down a list of techniques that might work for you.

Step 3: Put your stress-management techniques into practice

Choose one or two techniques from your list and try them out the next time you feel stressed. Make sure to give each technique enough time to see if it really helps you.

Step 4: Reflect on your results

Think about how well each technique worked for you. Did it help you feel less stressed? Did it make the stress go away completely? Write down your thoughts and feelings about each technique.

CHAPTER 10.

NATURE PRESERVATION AND ENVIRONMENTAL AWARENESS

Nature preservation and environmental awareness are important topics that everyone should learn about. The world we live in is full of amazing and unique plants, animals, and ecosystems that all work together to create a balanced and healthy environment. However, due to human activities, this balance is being disrupted, and many species are becoming endangered or even extinct.

It is crucial for us to learn about the environment and how we can help preserve it for future generations. We can start by reducing our impact on the environment, such as turning off the lights when we leave a room or taking shorter showers to conserve water. Another way to help is by recycling, which means reusing materials instead of throwing them away. This can help reduce the amount of waste that ends up in landfills and oceans.

Another way to support nature preservation is to learn about the different ecosystems and habitats in our area, and how to protect them. This might include planting trees, participating in clean-up events, or supporting organizations that work to protect the environment.

In addition to taking action to protect the environment, it is important to also raise awareness about these issues. This can be done by talking to friends and family, participating in environmental events, or sharing information online. By spreading the word, we can encourage others to join us in our efforts to protect the environment and preserve the beauty of nature.

In conclusion, nature preservation and environmental awareness are important topics that we should all learn about. By taking action and spreading awareness, we can help protect the environment and ensure a healthy and balanced world for generations to come.

Basic Animal Care:

Understanding the basics of animal care, including feeding, grooming, and providing basic medical attention.

Animal care is an important aspect of responsible pet ownership and can be a fun and rewarding experience. Whether you have a pet dog, cat, or even a small animal like a hamster, taking care of an animal requires time, effort, and patience.

First, it is important to understand the needs of the animal you are caring for. Different animals have different requirements, such as food, exercise, and living conditions. For example, dogs need daily walks, plenty of playtime, and a balanced diet, while hamsters require a cage that is the appropriate size for them, a place to hide, and a source of fresh food and water.

Second, it is essential to keep your pet healthy. Regular visits to the veterinarian can help identify any health problems early, and proper hygiene such as regular grooming and cleaning can prevent illnesses from spreading.

Third, playing with and bonding with your pet is a crucial aspect of animal care. This can help establish trust and a positive relationship, and can also provide mental and physical stimulation for your pet.

Finally, it is important to educate yourself about the proper way to handle and care for your pet. This can be done by reading books, asking a veterinarian, or seeking advice from other pet owners.

In conclusion, taking care of an animal is a big responsibility, but it can be a fun and educational experience for you. By understanding the needs of your pet, keeping them healthy, playing and bonding with them, and educating yourself, you can provide a loving and nurturing home for your furry friend.

EXERCISE ACTIVITY 16

EXERCISE ACTIVITY 16
"NATURE PRESERVATION ACTIVITY"

Objective:

To educate children on nature preservation skills.

Instructions

Step 1:
Go for a walk in a park or any green area near you.

Step 2:
Observe the different types of plants, animals, and insects that you see.

Step 3:
Pick up any litter you see on the ground and put it in the trash.

Step 4:
Think of ways you can help preserve nature, such as planting trees, reducing the use of plastic, or conserving energy.

Step 5:
Draw or write about what you have learned and what you can do to help preserve nature.

CHAPTER 11.

BASIC COMPUTER SKILLS

Basic computer skills and coding are important skills to learn in today's digital age. With technology playing an increasingly important role in our lives, it is essential that young children start to become familiar with computers and the basics of coding.

Computers are everywhere and can be used for a variety of tasks, such as playing games, doing homework, or even making new friends online. By learning basic computer skills, you can become more confident in using computers, and will be better equipped to handle the challenges of the future.

Since computers are now an integral part of our daily lives, it is crucial that you learn about them from an early age. You should be conversant with the following fundamental computing abilities:

Basic navigation: You should be able to operate the keyboard and mouse, launch and shut down programs, and save and retrieve files.

Internet safety: It is important to know how to use the internet safely by not disclosing personal information and not installing malicious software.

Word processing: You should be able to use word processing programs like Microsoft Word to produce and edit simple documents like letters.

Digital file organization: It is crucial to know how to organize their digital files, including how to move files around, create folders, and back up important information.

Email: You should know how to send and receive emails as well as how to use the fundamental functions, such as adding attachments and subject lines.

You will have a strong foundation to build on as you learn more about computers and use them in your daily lives thanks to these fundamental computing skills.

BASIC CODING:

Understanding the basics of coding and how it can be applied in various fields.

In our technologically advanced society, knowing how to code is a crucial ability. Writing instructions in a language a computer can comprehend and utilize to carry out various tasks is known as programming.

Coding may be a fascinating and entertaining approach for you to learn about technology. You can acquire the following fundamental principles about coding:

Sequences: To program a computer to carry out a task, we must write instructions in a precise sequence. It is crucial to comprehend the order in which instructions are issued because this is referred to as a sequence.

Loops: In coding, a loop is a repeating pattern. They save the computer from having to repeatedly write the same instructions in order to complete a task.

Variables: In a computer program, variables are used to store data and information. Then, you can utilize this information to carry out various actions and come to conclusions.

If-then statements: These are a fundamental building block of coding. They are used to base judgements on certain circumstances. The computer, for instance, will carry out one activity while it is raining outside but another when it is sunny.

Learning to code can be done in a variety of methods, such as through online tutorials, seminars, and games. It is crucial to discover a learning strategy that suits you and to enjoy the process.

In conclusion, learning to code is a useful ability that can aid in the development of young children's problem-solving and critical thinking abilities. You can begin exploring the fascinating world of coding and technology with a little practice and effort.

EXERCISE ACTIVITY 17

EXERCISE ACTIVITY 17
"CODING IN A PROGRAMMING LANGUAGE"

Objective:

To educate children on nature preservation skills.

Instructions

Welcome to the world of coding! Today, we are going to learn how to program a computer to do something cool.

Step 1:
Open a text editor on your computer.

Step 2:
Type in the following code:
print("Hello, World!")

Step 3:
Save the file as "HelloWorld.py".

Step 4:
Open the terminal and navigate to the directory where the file is saved.

Step 5:
Type "python HelloWorld.py" and press enter.

Congratulations! You just wrote your first program. This program is called a "Hello World" program and it is a great way to get started with coding. Now, let us try changing the text in the program.

Replace "Hello, World!" with your name. Save the file and run it again. See what happens!

ONE LAST THING

Author's note:

Thank you so much for reading this book. Once you read this book, I want your honest review and feedback so that I can improve the book. I take all the reviews and feedback seriously and will try my best to make this book even better.

Please consider leaving a review on Amazon.

CLICK the LINK below to leave a review.

Thank you for your support!

- Rafiq Khan, MD, PhD

Scan the QR Code below to give feedback!

Made in United States
Orlando, FL
22 September 2023

37162021R00109